501 ASTONISHING FACTS

Sanjeev Garg

Illustrated by: Udayshankar

PUSTAK MAHAL®
DELHI • BANGALORE • MUMBAI • PATNA • HYDERABAD

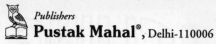

Publishers
Pustak Mahal®, Delhi-110006

J-3/16 , Daryaganj, New Delhi-110002
☎ 23276539, 23272783, 23272784 • *Fax:* 011-23260518
E-mail: info@pustakmahal.com • *Website:* www.pustakmahal.com

Branch Offices
Bangalore: ☎ 22234025
E-mail: pmblr@sancharnet.in • pustak@sancharnet.in
Mumbai: ☎ 22010941
E-mail: rapidex@bom5.vsnl.net.in
Patna: ☎ 3094193 • *Telefax:* 0612-2302719
E-mail: rapidexptn@rediffmail.com
Hyderabad: *Telefax:* 040-24737290
E-mail: pustakmahalhyd@yahoo.co.in

© Pustak Mahal, 6686, Khari Baoli, Delhi-110006

ISBN 81-223-0354-4

Edition : 2005

Printed at : Hi-Zeal Graphics, Delhi

PREFACE

In our daily life, we see or hear from others about many fascinating things. Sometimes, they appear totally unbelievable. This book presents 501 such Astonishing Facts.

The book has been presented in ten chapters. These highlight the most peculiar aspects of the earth, universe, human body, animals, birds, plants, people, places, science, technology and many others. The book also shows some additional items. Most of the facts have been illustrated fairly well.

The book has been written in a popular easy appealing language for the common readers, especially children.

I hope it will be appreciated by all readers.

Sanjeev Garg

Contents

1. ASTONISHING PLANET EARTH

Booming Sound
Loud booming sounds are produced in deserts when sand slips down the steep faces of the dunes.

How Cold
The average temperature at South Pole is -50°C. In 1983, Russian Vostok Station, east of the South Pole recorded the lowest temperature of -89.2°C.

Magnetic Poles
The North Magnetic Pole is about 1600 km from the true North Pole, while the South Magnetic Pole is about 2570 km from the South Pole.

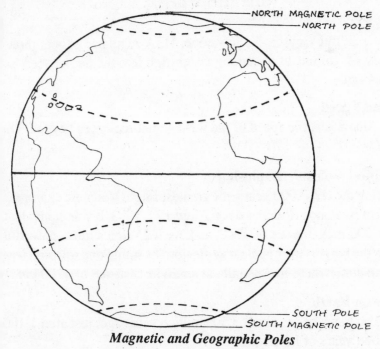

Magnetic and Geographic Poles

Old Faithful Geyser.

Geyser
Old Faithful Geyser, Yellowstone, USA regularly shoots thousands of gallons of streaming water high into the air between 37 and 46 m.

Wind Speed
On Antarctica, the speed of the wind sometimes goes beyond 300 km/hr.

Loudest Volcanic Explosion
During the last 3,000 years, the greatest single Volcanic explosion was of Krakatoa (Indonesia) on August 27, 1883. It was equivalent to 1,500 megatonnes of TNT, making it 25 times more powerful than the biggest ever nuclear explosion. Its sound of explosion was heard somewhere in Australia at a remote distance of 4700 km.

Life on Earth
Life on Earth began about 3,500 million years ago, just after 1,100 million years of its origin.

River Nile

Among the 50 big rivers of the world, Nile is 6,650 km long and Amazon 6,450 km long.

Desert Without Rain

Atacama desert of Chile never had any rainfall for about 400 years until 1971. It is considered as the driest plateau across the world.

Sailing Around the Earth

It is possible to sail all the way around the Earth on latitude 60° south.

Rock of Ages

The oldest known rocks, found in Western Australia are about 3,200 million years old — about 300 million years younger than the planet itself.

International Date-line

A traveller crossing the International date-line can actually leave the same day of a week twice.

International Date-line.

Water Cycle.

Water Cycle
Water which has been evaporated today from the oceans will reach back after a period of 1,000 years.

Lowest Hill
The lowest hill of 15 ft height is shown on the official map of Syria. Its name is Bukit Thompson.

Ice Thickness
The greatest ice thickness in Antarctic region has been measured to be 4,776 metres i.e., about 3 miles.

Tides
The greatest tides occur in the bay of Fundy.

Underground Lake
Most of the lakes are on the land, but there is one under the ground. Its name is Lost Sea. It is in the USA and was discovered in 1905.

Sand Dunes
Sand Dunes in Sahara Desert can attain heights of 1,400 ft. equivalent to many mountains of the Earth.

Oceans
We see land everywhere on the Earth, but it is a planet whose 71 per cent land mass is covered with water.

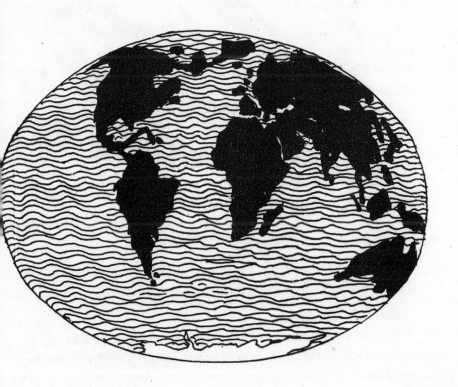

Land and Water on Earth

An Iceberg.

Iceberg
In 1956, an iceberg from Antarctica came on record-335 km long and 97 km wide much larger than the size of Delhi.

Antarctic Ice Melt
If the ice of Antarctic continent melts, the level of water in the oceans will become so high that the whole world will become flooded.

Sahara
Sahara desert occupies about 1/8 area of the land. It is about 9 million square kilometres.

Natural Bridge.

Natural Bridge

Man has made beautiful and long bridges all over the world, but Nature has made bridges of its own. Such a highest natural bridge exists in Sinkiang, China, which is 312 m height with a span of 45 m.

Sea Level

Due to the global warming effect, the level of water in the Caspian Sea has started rising. This is a warning to human race that any day, the continents may become over-flooded.

Lowest Point on Earth	:	Dead Sea
Longest River	:	Nile
Largest Desert	:	Sahara
Deepest Lake	:	Lake Baikal
Largest Island	:	Greenland

Mount Everest.

Highest Peak	: Mount Everest- 8848 m.
Largest Sea	: South China Sea
Largest and deepest Ocean	: Pacific
Largest Continent	: Asia

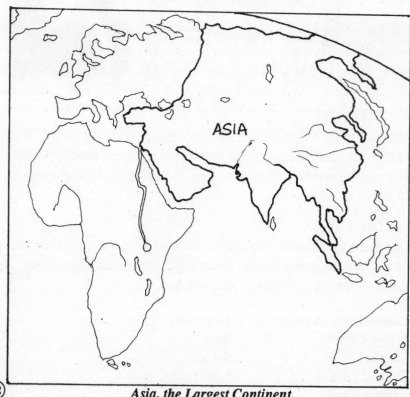

Asia, the Largest Continent.

Angel Falls.

Newest Island	:	Lateiki
Highest Waterfall	:	Angel Falls
Largest Delta	:	Ganga & Brahmaputra in Bangladesh
Largest Salt Water Lake	:	Caspian Sea
Largest Fresh Water Lake	:	Lake Superior
Longest Glacier	:	Lambert Glacier
Surface Area of Earth	:	510,101,000 sq. km.

■ ■

2. UNBELIEVABLE FACTS ABOUT UNIVERSE

Giant Star
Antares star is about 420 million kilometres in diameter, which is 300 times the width of the sun.

Black Hole
The gravitational field inside a black hole is so strong that it can swallow anything in the universe, even a passing star and its light. If a book weighing 1 kg is brought to within 6 m of a black hole, it would weigh a million million tonnes.

Lunar Scars
The surface of the moon is pitted with craters of all sizes up to 250 km in diameter. These have been created by meteorites smashing into the surface long ago.

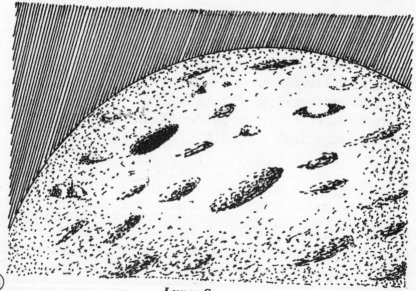

Lunar Scars.

Thunderstorm.

Thunderstorms
At any given moment, there are about 1,800 thunderstorms raging around the world, generating between them about 6,000 flashes of lightning every minute.

Largest Volcano
The largest volcano in the solar system is on Mars Olympus Moons, 600 km wide and 24,000 m high, is nearly three times higher than Mt. Everest.

Sun's Revolutions
So far, sun has orbited the Galaxy 20 times, because it takes 220 million years to orbit the centre of the Galaxy.

Power Houses
Quassars are stupendous power houses. They give out as much energy as hundreds of galaxies from a volume of space only a light year across.

Sea of Rains
The Sea of Rains is situated on the moon. Amazingly it has no water.

Meteorite Hit
A meteorite in 1954 badly bruised a woman in Alabama, USA.

Heavenly Missile
In the morning of June 30, 1908, a brilliant fireball blazed through skies over Siberia, exploding above the stony Tunguska river with a force of a 12 megaton bomb. It knocked down trees for up to 30 km around, set the forest ablaze and caused shock waves like an earthquake. It was perhaps the fragment from the head of a comet, about 100-metre across and one million tonnes in weight.

Halley's Comet.

Halley's Comet
Halley's comet is seen after every 76 years in the sky. It was last seen in the year 1986.

Space Record
Astronauts can stay in space for a few days but surprisingly *Valley Ryumin* of USSR has stayed in space in *Salyut-6* for 362 days — almost a year.

Sun.

Life of Sun
The Sun is a 5 billion years old star and is supposed to remain exist for another 5 billion years.

Jupiter
Jupiter planet is mostly made of gases.

Sirus
Sirus is called Dog Star.

Dog in Space
The first living being to go into space was a dog named *Laika* on 3rd November 1957.

Planet's Name from a God
The planet Jupiter – the largest in the solar system – gets its name from Rome's supreme God, Jupiter.

Sun's Size
109 Earths would fit side by side across the diameter of the sun.

A Chip of the Moon
A tiny slice of moon rock is sealed in the stained glass window dedicated to scientists and technicians in Washington Cathedral, USA. The rock was brought to Earth by Apollo-astronauts in 1969.

Planet that Spins Backwards
Unlike other planets in the solar system, Venus spins not from west to east, but from east to west.

The Fastest Moon
A new and tiny moon of Jupiter revolves round the planet in just over seven hours — making it the fastest moon in the solar system.

Star Counting
One can count all the visible stars in the sky in about one hour.

Meteors
More than 75 million meteors enter the earth's atmosphere every day, but they disintegrate before hitting the ground.

Star Counting.

Fire Ball

A fire ball over Sumava 10,000 times brighter than moon was photographed in 1974.

Mars

Mars is called Red planet because its surface is red.

Talking in Space

We cannot talk in space as we do so on Earth, because there is no medium to carry sound waves.

Talking in Space – Impossible.

Meteor Shower

On November 1966, there occurred a meteor shower in USA at a rate of 2300 per minute for a period of about 20 minutes.

Meteorite Crater

A crater 241 km in diameter and 805 m deep was created in Antarctica by a meteorite.

Highest Number of Eclipses

So far the highest number of solar and lunar eclipses in a year have been recorded in 1935. In this year, there were five solar and two lunar eclipses.

Pluto

Pluto is the smallest and coldest planet among all the ten planets. (19)

Moon Rock.

Moon's Oldest Rock
Astronauts have brought rocks from the surface of moon which are estimated to be 4720 million years old.

Sirus
Sirus star is much much brighter than the sun. In fact, no star is as bright as Sirus.

Polaris
The North Star or Polaris always appears in the same position in the northern sky, because it is almost exactly above the North Pole.

North Star

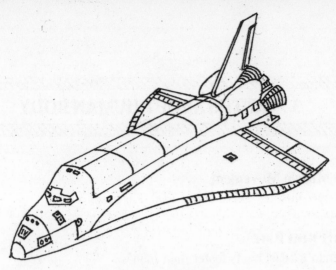

Space Shuttle.

Cost of Space Shuttle

The cost of space shuttle programme is about $ 9.0 billion. It is equivalent to spending about $ 2.0 for every man, woman and child in the world. A new space shuttle costs about $ 600 million.

Weight on Sun and Moon

A person of 60 kg weight will barely weigh 10 kg on moon, but 1,680 kg on the sun.

Sun–Moon Atmospheric Variation.

3. TRUTHS ABOUT HUMAN BODY

Eye Muscle Movement
Our eye muscles move about 1,00,000 times a day.

Heart Beat Rate
Woman's heart beats faster than man's.

Saliva
Man's salivary glands secrete 1 to 1.5 litres of saliva every day.

Wonder Brain
Messages from the brain to the different body parts are sent at a rate of 240 miles per hour.

Human Eye
The weight of each human eye is about 1.5 ounces.

Left and Right Feet
Our right foot is slightly longer than the left foot.

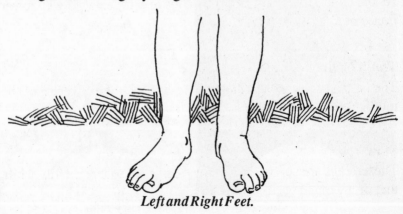

Left and Right Feet.

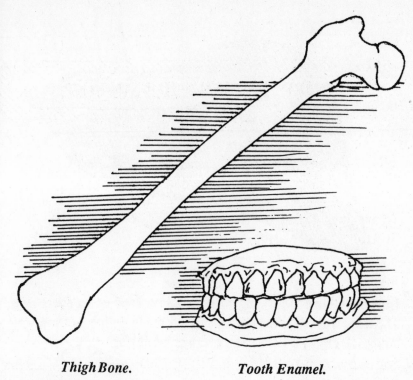

Thigh Bone.   *Tooth Enamel.*

Longest Bone

The longest human bone is femur or thigh bone which is 48 cm long. It is so strong that it can support 30 times the weight of a man.

Number of Bones

Most human adults have 206 bones, but a new born baby has 330. As the child grows, some of the bones join together to give fewer bones in total.

Tooth Enamel

The hardest substance in the body is enamel – the covering of the tooth.

Skin

The average area of the skin of the man is 1.8 square metres, while that of a woman is 1.6 square metres.

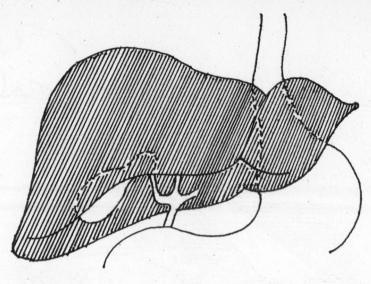

Liver.

Largest Gland
The largest gland in the human body is the liver that measures 21.5 cm by 19 cm by 14 cm in an average adult (Fig. 3.3).

Kidneys
Our kidneys filter about 120 millilitres of blood per minute. The entire blood supply is filtered about 30 times a day.

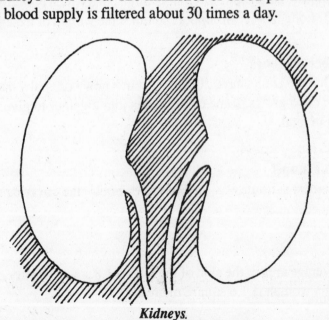

Kidneys.

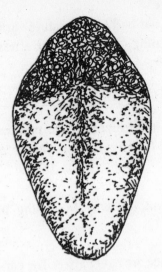

Tongue.

Tongue
Tongue is the only muscle in our body that is attached at one end only.

Number of Menstruations
An average woman can expect to menstruate about 450 times between the commencement of menstruation at the age of 12 and the menopause at the age of 50.

Number of Ova
A baby girl is born with her whole life-time supply of about two million tiny unripe eggs. Only about one egg in 2500 will ever ripen and leave an ovary.

Number of Sperms
On an average, a man produces more than 500 million sperms every day. Sperms that are ejaculated from the penis soon decay and are absorbed back into body.

Brain
Our brain can store, recognise and remember 10,000 different odours.

Body Temperature

It is surprising that our body temperature varies during the day. It is lowest in the morning, rises in the late afternoon and falls again when we sleep.

Blood

Blood takes barely one minute to be pumped around the body through arteries and return back to the heart through veins.

Muscle Work

Our muscles only work one way, by pulling, but they never push.

Face

Both sides of your face are never alike. The ears are not at the same level, one eye is stronger than the other and the right ear is usually higher than the left.

Elements

There are 24 elements in the human body of which hydrogen content is 63% whereas oxygen is 25.5%.

Brisk Walk

Brisk walking uses eight times as many calories as writing.

Brisk Walking and Writing.

Teeth Cleaning
Brushing your teeth with salt cleans them as effectively as brushing them with tooth paste.

The Hair Facts
On an average, both men and women have a total of about 5 million hairs on their bodies. Fair-haired people have slightly more than the average, redheads slightly fewer. The only areas that are totally hairless are the lips, the palms of the hands, the soles of the feet, the sides of the toes and fingers and the upper part of the ends of the fingers and toes.

The Mighty Snore
The sound of a snore (up to 69 decibels) can be almost as loud as the noise of a pneumatic drill (70-90 decibels).

Child's Height
Doubling a child's height on his second birthday gives a close estimate of his final adult height. A boy of two is 49.5 per cent of his adult height, whereas a girl of two is 52.8 per cent of her adult height.

Sun-tan in the Shade
It is possible to get a tan or sunburn even on a cloudy day, because about 80 per cent of the ultraviolet rays from the sun get through the cloud.

Sun-tan in the Shade.

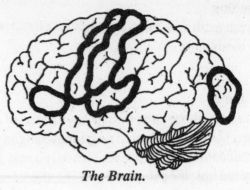

The Brain.

Brain Weight

The brain accounts for about 3 per cent of body weight, but it uses 20 per cent of all the oxygen we breathe, 20 per cent of the calories in the food we eat and about 15 per cent of the body blood supply.

Nail Growth

In a period of about six months, each of our finger nail or toe nail grows from its base to the tip.

Blood Volume

During pregnancy, a woman's blood volume can increase up to 50 per cent to a total of 6.75 litres.

Bone Strength

Human bone is as strong as granite in supporting weight. A block of the size of a match box can support one tonne of weight.

Muscles and Joints

The adult human body contains approximately 650 muscles, over 100 joints, 100,000 km of blood vessels and 13,000 million nerve cells.

Body Water

The body of the average adult contains 45 litres of water — about 65 per cent of his weight.

Number of Sperms

A man's testicles manufacture 10 million new sperm cells a day — enough in six months to populate the entire world.

Acids in Human Body

The stomach's digestive acids are strong enough to dissolve zinc. But, the cells in the stomach lining are renewed so quickly — 500,000 cells are replaced every minute and the entire lining every three days — that the acids don't have time to dissolve the lining.

Pulse Rate

The average pulse rate is 70 -72 beats per minute at rest for adult males and 78-82 for adult females. The rate can increase to as much as 200 per minute during violent exercise.

Capillaries in Lungs

The lungs contain a total of 300,000 million capillaries — tiny blood vessels — which would stretch to 2,400 km (1500 miles), if laid end to end.

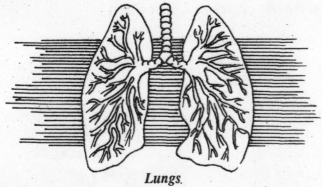

Lungs.

Heartbeat

The heart beats more than 2000 million times during the average human life span and during that period it will pump around 500 million litres of blood.

Diet

The average person in the West eats 50 tonnes of food and drinks 50,000 litres (11,000 gallons) of liquid during his life.

Largest Organ

The body's largest organ is the skin. In an adult man, it covers about 1.9m², a woman has about 1.6m² on average, each person sheds about 18 kg of skin during his lifetime.

Internal Ear

Internal ear maintains the equilibrium of the body.

Growth at Night

We grow by about 8 mm every night when asleep, but shrink to the former height on the following day. During the day, the cartilage discs in the spine are squeezed like sponges by gravity while we sit or stand. But at night, when we lie down to sleep, the pressure is relieved and the discs swell again. For the same reason, astronauts can be temporarily 50 mm (2 inches) taller, after a long space flight.

Human Kidneys

Each kidney in a human body contains some one million individual filters, and between them the two kidneys filter an average of about 1.2 litres of blood in a minute. The waste products are expelled as urine at the rate of about 1.4 litres a day.

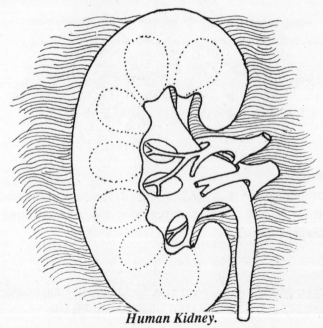

Human Kidney.

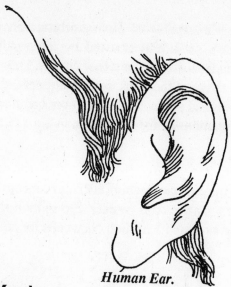
Human Ear.

Smallest Muscle
The smallest human muscle is in the ear. It is a little over 1 mm long.

Muscle Movement
The focussing muscles of the eye move about 100,000 times a day. To give the leg muscle the same exercise would involve at least 80 km (50 miles) walking a day.

Thumb
The thumb is so important to the human dexterity that a larger proportion of the brain is devoted to control it than to control the whole of the chest and abdomen.

The Poisonous Oxygen
If pure oxygen is breathed at more than two and half times atmospheric pressure, it can act as a poison.

The Super Strength Hormone
The hormone *adrenalin*, produced naturally in the body under stress, has the power to increase a person's strength far beyond its usual limits.

Tasting, Tasting

The human tongue is capable of distinguishing only four basic tastes. The tongue's surface is covered by thousands of nerve endings — taste buds — divided into four groups. Those on the tip sense sweetness; those at the back sense bitterness; those at the sides sense saltiness and sourness. All the more complex tastes are made up of combinations of the basic four.

Retina

The retina inside the eye covers about 650 mm² and contains some 137 million light sensitive cells besides 130 million rod cells for black and white vision, and 7 million cone cells for colour vision.

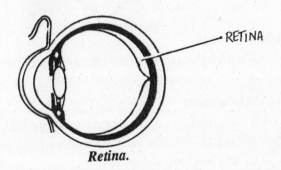

Retina.

Pinta Power

Half a litre of milk a day provides, on average one sixth of a person's daily energy requirement.

Radioactive People

Every human body is naturally radioactive. It is so, since the body contains a little amount of the radioactive isotope Potassium-40 and Carbon-14, which is absorbed by living organisms from atmosphere.

Half and Half

There are 46 chromosomes in the living cell of a human being. But the sex cells, the female egg and male sperm, each have only 23 chromosomes. They fuse at conception to make cell containing 46 chromosomes, half from each partner.

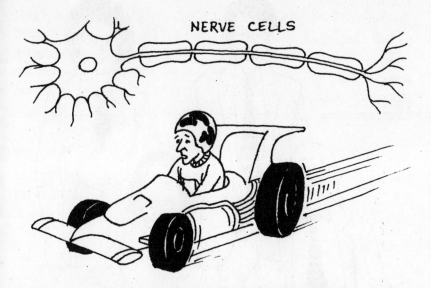

NERVE CELLS

Speed of Nerve Impulses Equal to Racing Cars.

Nerve Impulses

Nerve impulses—to and from the brain, travel as fast as some racing cars. The fastest impulses recorded have travelled at nearly 290 km/hr.

Brain

Brain has no sensation of pain even when it is cut.

Tallest and Heaviest.

Tallest Woman	2.46 m
Tallest Man	2.72 m
Heaviest Man	635 kg
Heaviest Woman	400 kg
Longest Bone	Thigh Bone or Femur Bone
Smallest Bone	Stirrup in the Ear
Largest Muscle	Gluteus
Smallest Muscle	Stapedius
Largest Organ	Brain

4. FASCINATING WORLD OF ANIMALS

Crocodile Tears
Crocodiles shed tears when they eat a meal.

Egg Laying Mammals
Mammals give birth to young ones, but there are some like *spiny anteater* and *platypus* which lay eggs.

Sloth.

Upside Down
Sloth is a strange animal which spends its entire life hanging upside down from the branches of trees.

Cheetah.

Cheetah Speed

Cheetah can run to short distances with speed up to 96 km/hr. This is the fastest running animal.

Strange Eyes

The eyes of the giant squid are very strange. They measure 40 cm across. These creatures live in dark and gloomy conditions, that is why, they have big eyes to see clearly in poor visible conditions.

Strange Eyes

Sea horse has strange eyes, by which it can focus in two different directions at the same time.

Mammoth Fish

Whale shark measures 18 metre. It is the world's biggest fish.

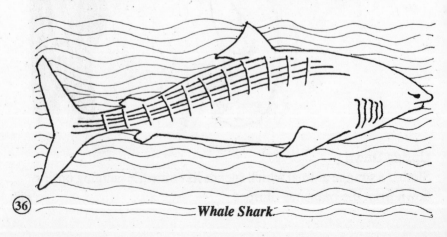

Whale Shark.

Pollution
Pollution is affecting the animal world so badly that their dwindling rate may go as high as one per minute by the year 2000.

Racoon
Racoon is such an interesting animal that it washes its food before eating.

Light Producing Fish
There are about 600 marine organisms which produce light from their bodies. Angler fish and lantern fish are two such fishes.

Porpoise
Porpoise is so intelligent sea animal that it can copy many actions of humans. It can imitate the voice of a man and even can laugh.

Musk
Musk is obtained from the gland of an animal called musk deer.

Musk Deer.

Three Hearts
Most of the living beings have only one heart, but cuttle fish is a strange one which has three hearts.

Cow
Surprisingly, the cow has four stomachs.

Lemmings
Lemmings are strange animals. When their number in an area increases beyond a certain limit, they jump into the sea and commit suicide.

Strange Rat
Kangaroo rat can survive over its life without drinking water. It meets its requirement of water by eating the roots of some desert plants.

Kangaroo
Kangaroo can jump to a height of more than 10 ft which is roughly one and half times the record high jump of an athlete.

Kangaroo.

Horses
There are 75,000,000 horses in the world.

Killi Fish
Killi fish's life span is very small, surprisingly only eight months.

Lady Bird
The lady bird is not a bird, it is a beetle.

Strange Frog
Gastric frog of Australia gives birth to its young ones through its mouth.

Snails
Snails have 14175 teeth laid along 135 rows on their tongue.

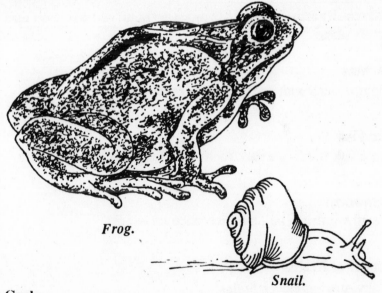

Frog.

Snail.

Cock
Onagadori cocks are only 45 cm in length, but their tails are up to 14 m long.

White Tigers
All the zoo-bred white tigers of the world come from Rewa, Madhya Pradesh, in India.

A Butterfly.

Butterfly
A butterfly has 12,000 eyes.

Botfly
Botfly can fly at the speed of 818 miles per hour, which is faster than a Jet air plane.

Dolphins
Dolphins sleep with one of its eyes open.

Gold Fish
If gold fish is left in a dark room for a long time, it turns white.

Earthworm
An earthworm can pull ten times its own weight.

Number of Brains
A silkworm has eleven brains.

Gopher
The gopher can run backward almost as fast as forward.

Colorodo Beetles
A pair of colorodo beetles can multiply up to 60 million in a year.

Milk
The colour of milk of Himalayan yak is pink.

Bees
One kilogram of honey is obtained from 4 million flowers by bees.

Whale
A blue whale eats about 3 tonnes of food every day, but at the same time it can live without food for 6 months.

Snails
Snails surprisingly can sleep for 3 to 4 years continuously.

Insects
Some insects can live about a year after their heads have been separated.

Cats
All cats born in Thailand are white in colour.

Horse
Horses can sleep in standing posture.

Horse Sleeping in Standing Posture.

Transparent Body
The Indian glass perch has a completely transparent body.

Porcupine
A small porcupine can kill a grown up lion.

Red Sweat
When a hippopotamus gets excited, its sweat becomes red.

Crow
Crow is the most clever of all birds.

Dogs
Surprisingly, dogs are descendants of wolves.

Wolf.

Dog.

Marmot
Marmot squeals so loudly that the voice can be heard at a distance of 3 km.

Horse Teeth
A male horse has 40 teeth.

Mule
A mule is a cross between a male ass and a mare (female horse).

Quelea.

Quelea

About ten thousand million red-billed quelea live in Africa. It is the most numerous backboned land animal.

Giraffe

Giraffe's tongue is such that the animal can clean its ears with it.

Animals and Plants

The Earth has over 1,200,000 species of animals, 300,000 species of plants and 100,000 other species.

House Fly Eyes

A house fly has big compound eyes, each having about 4000 tiny lenses.

Turtle

A green turtle performed a record journey from South America to Africa. It swam a distance of 5900 km.

Blue Whale

The length of blue whale is about 10 times that of a Fiat car. It measures 33.6 m in length and weighs 190 tonnes.

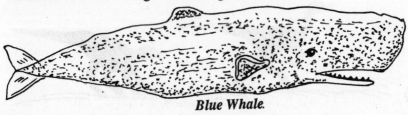

Blue Whale.

Wolf Spider Eyes.

Honey Bee Eyes.

Strange Spider

Wolf spider has eight eyes, while a honey bee has five eyes (three simple and two compound).

Cow

In Ontario, Canada, a cow was sold for $ 1.3 million.

Kangaroo

An adult kangaroo stands about 2 metre in height and weighs about 50 kg, but a baby kangaroo at the time of birth is only 2.5 mm in length and weighs only 1 gm.

Tape Worm

Tape worm found in human intestines may be 60 ft in length.

Branchiosaurus

Branchiosaurus was so large a dinosaur which weighed 100,000 pounds, 40 feet tall and 80 feet long.

Dinosaur

The fierce dinosaur was the Tyrannosaurus which had sixty long and sharp teeth, used to attack and eat other dinosaurs.

Dinosaurs.

Wolf Spider

The female wolf spider carries her young ones on her back, but if one falls off she will not stop.

Pearl

Pearl is made by a sea creature called Oyster inside its body.

Honey-bee

To collect just an ounce (28 gm) of honey, a bee may have to fly about 130 km.

A Honey Bee.

Flying Fish

The flying fish can glide over half a minute. Sometimes, it reaches up to the decks of ships.

Lizard Tail

A lizard can escape after leaving its tail behind. After some time, the tail regenerates.

Howling Monkey

Howling monkey is the noisiest of all, the howls of which can be heard up to four miles.

Hearing

Crickets hear through their knees, whereas cicadas through their stomachs.

Colour Blindness
Except man, apes and chimpanzees, most mammals are colour blind i.e. they cannot distinguish between colours.

Ant
Ants can pull loads 300 times their own weight.

An Ant.

Australian Dingo
All dogs can bark, but Australian dog dingo cannot.

Horse Anger
Horses show aggression by laying back their ears.

Wolves Attack
Due to the severe cold in 1592, the starving wolves dared to enter Vienna town in Austria and attacked both men and live-stock, at random.

Three Names
Male seals are called bulls, females are called cows but their young ones are called pups.

Seals.

Razor Teeth
The Pirankes fish of Amazon have immensely strong jaws and razor sharp teeth as long as one foot. They have such razor sharp teeth that they reduce 45 kg capybara, the largest rodent in the world to a skeleton in less than 60 seconds.

Tortoise Sentenced to Death
In July 1981, a tortoise was sentenced to death for murder. In the eastern village of Kyuasine, the tribal elders formally condemned the tortoise following their suspicion of causing the deaths of six people apparently through magic. However, instead of executing the tortoise, it was chained to a tree. Later on, it was freed after the governent promised an official enquiry into the unusual deaths.

Python
A python can swallow a bear of 90 kg weight.

Ant that Eats Itself
The queen of the black garden ant feeds partly on its own wing muscles.

May Fly
May fly's lifespan is only one day.

Male Mother
Sea horse is one of the few species in the animal world in which male gives birth to the young. The male has a special broad-pouch on its abdomen into which the female lays eggs.

Four-eyed Fish
Tropical American fish has four eyes.

Pigmy Goby
Pigmy goby is so small that it is only 8 mm long.

Non-stop Flight
Many species of butterfly by their mere wing-power can travel 1000 km without a refuelling stop. Some have been known to fly right across the Atlantic ocean.

Giraffe's Neck
Giraffe's neck is very long, but surprisingly it has only seven bones in it, the same as we do.

The Big Sleep
The North American wood chuck spends as much as eight months each year asleep.

Whale of a Brain
Sperm whales have the heaviest brain of any animal, it can weigh more than 9 kg, six times larger than an average human brain.

The Nose Knows
Although, most dogs have poor eyesight, they possess a superb sense of smell.

Vision from Skin
Some insects are able to see light apparently through their skin. Experiments with the caterpillars of moths and butterflies show even with their eyes covered, they are still sensitive to light.

Double Milk
The red kangaroo can produce two different kinds of milk at the same time from adjacent teats.

Killed by a Tortoise
The Greek dramatist Aeschylus was killed, when an eagle dropped a trotoise on the play wright's bald head.

It's a Dog's Life
The only living creature known to have been killed by an extraterrestrial object was a dog, struck dead by a small meteorite.

Insects
Every year about one thousand species of insects are discovered.

Ants
There are about one thousand billion ants living on the Earth. This number is roughly 200 times more than the human population of the world.

Insect Blood
Insect blood has no colour. If any insect has red blood, it will be the blood of another animal on which it is feeding.

Tiger
Tiger and lion are the members of cat family.

Elephant Pollination
The largest flower, Rafflesia is pollinated by elephant.

Squirrels
Squirrels use their tails as parachutes, while leaping to the ground.

Deer
Deers use their tails to convey signals to others in their herd.

Termite Queen
A termite queen can produce over 30,000 eggs in one day.

Grasshoppers
Grasshoppers sing by rubbing pegs on their hind legs.

Kangaroo
The kangaroo uses its thick tail as a fifth limb.

Leech
A leech after sucking the blood for 20 minutes increases its body weight five-fold and it hardly needs another meal up to a year.

Dog-spectators
A film called, "The Dog that Saved Hollywood" was shown to an audience of 100 dogs.

Camel
In a sandstorm, the camel can close its nose.

Cat's Sleep
Human beings sleep for about eight hours in every twenty-four hours, but cats sleep for about sixteen hours in twenty-four hours.

Dangerous to Touch
Electric eel can produce electricity, which is sufficient to light up ten bulbs. Its surface potential can measure up to 500 volts (D.C.) and is sufficient to kill any swimmer who touches the fish.

Big Baby
The weight of a blue whale baby at the time of birth is about 3000 kg i.e. 3 tonnes and in a span of two years the weight becomes 26,000 kg. No other creature grows so quickly.

Scorpion Size
The largest species of Scorpion found in India measures 25 cms from the end of the sting to the tips of the pincers. If it stings, the man dies in about four hours.

Busy Bee
A single honey bee travels a distance of over 75,000 km to make 500 gm of honey.

Muscle Record
Each Human being has 650 muscles; but strange enough, a caterpillar has 2700 muscles, four times as many as we have.

Astonishing Crabs

A giant relative of the hermit crab finds food not in the water as in the case of ordinary crabs but in the trees. The robber crab *birgars latro* lives on Indian Oceans and on the Islands of the south west Pacific.

Dimetrodon

Dimetrodon was a mammal like reptile with a sail on its back. This acted like a radiator to cool the body of the animal.

Largest frog	Goliath frog
Largest animal	Blue whale
Largest fish	Whale shark
Largest snake	Anaconda
Fastest running animal	Cheetah
Slowest animal	Snail
Smallest animal	Pigmy shrew
Tallest mammal	Giraffe
Largest marsupial	Kangaroo
Longest survival	Tortoise
Heaviest land mammal	African elephant

■ ■

5. PECULIAR BIRDS

Strong Eggs
Eggs seem to break very easily, but they are really quite strong. Try to break a chicken's egg by squeezing its ends, you will find it almost impossible to break it this way.

Feather Weight
The humming bird is so small that it weighs less than the sphinx moth.

Mute Swan
Mute Swan is the heaviest flying bird. It weighs more than 18 kg.

Wonder Bird
Sooty Tern is a wonder bird that can fly for 3 to 4 years continuously.

Dangerous Bird
Cassowary is so dangerous a bird that it can kill a man or animal by tearing off with its dagger like claw.

Most Talkative
The world's most talkative bird is a female African parrot owned by Mrs. Lyn Logue of Seaford, Sussex, UK.

Feathers
The swan has over 25,000 feathers on its body.

Penguins.

Penguin
Penguin can dive down water to a depth of 266 metre and stay there for 18 minutes.

Ostrich Race
Ostrich races are held in Montrouge near Paris, France, with human jockey in the saddle and the birds attaining a speed of 40 miles per hour.

Tailor Bird
The Tailor bird makes its nest by sewing the edges of the leaves together. It uses its beak as needle and plant's fibres as thread.

Best Imitator
The mocking bird has the ability to imitate the songs of 40 different birds.

A Regular Visitor
Siberian Crane comes every year in winter to India from Siberia.

Woodpecker
The Woodpecker uses its long sticky tongue to eat ants.

Kiwi
Australian Kiwi is a peculiar bird which has no wings. It cannot even jump two feet.

Ostrich Egg

The size of the ostrich egg is almost equal to a watermelon. It is 20 cm long, 150 cm in diameter and weighs 1.78 kg. It can yield Omelettes for eight persons.

Arctic Tern

The Arctic Tern is such a bird which makes a round trip from North to South Pole covering a distance of 25,000 miles.

Turkey

One of the most strangely named birds is Turkey. It originated in North America and was taken to Europe in 1500s. When the birds were introduced in England around AD 1541, people thought they had come from Turkey and hence named.

Turkey.   *Bat.*

Bats

Bats can hear sounds in the frequency range of 1000 to 120,000 Hz and produce sounds 10,000 to 120,000 Hz.

Vampire Bat

Vampire bat sucks the blood of animals. It can even suck the blood of human beings.

Ducks

Ducks only lay eggs early in the morning.

Owl's Sight

An owl can see five times more than the human beings, because the number of rods and cones in the eyes of an owl are 10,000 per square mm; while this number is only 2,000 per square mm in human eyes. (55)

Strange Nest
Strangest nest probably once made by a sparrow in Switzerland consisted entirely of watch springs.

Swifts
European Swift is a bird which never touches ground. It eats, drinks, sleeps and even mates while flying.

Canaries
Only male Canaries can sing.

Diving Bird
The best diving bird is the Penguin. It can dive under water to a depth of 266 metres and stay there for 18 minutes.

Fastest Flier
The world's fastest flying bird is the Peregrine Falcon which can swoop on its prey at speeds of up to 350 km/hr.

Bats
Bats are the only flying mammals.

Weaver Nest
The weaver bird Baya weaves a pendulous, bottle shaped nest of arrows which is suspended by long fibrous strand or rope attached to the branch of a tree. The entrance is made through a narrow tunnel towards the end so that big birds cannot get in.

Condor

Osrich

Wondering
Albatross

Humming Bird

Arctic Tern

Largest Bird	:	Ostrich
Smallest Bird	:	Humming Bird
Heaviest Flying Bird	:	Mute Swan
Largest Flying Bird	:	Condor
Fastest Bird	:	Indian Swift
Longest Lived Bird	:	Andean Condor
Largest Egg	:	Osrich
Highest Flying	:	Egyptian Geese
Longest Flights	:	Arctic Tern
Largest Wing Span	:	Wondering Albatross
Fastest Swimmer	:	Penguin
Most Talkative	:	African Grey Parrot

Underground Nest

The oil bird of tropical South America rests and nests in underground caverns that are sometimes more than a kilometre from the open air.

Pink Colour

Flamingos owe their distinctive pink colouring to their diet.

Backward Flight
Humming bird can fly backwards.

Song Bird
Indian bird Shama is considered the best song bird of India.

Parrot
Parrot is the only bird that can move both the upper and lower parts of its beak.

Pebbles Eater
Ostrich eat pebbles to help digestion by grinding up the ingested food.

Head Rotation
The Owl can rotate its head by 180° on either side.

Life Span
Andean Condor can survive over 70 years.

Andean Condor

Highest Flying
Egyptian goose is the highest flying bird. An astronomer of Dehradun photographed it, when it was flying between 11 and 12 miles in the year 1919.

Bald Eagle
Bald Eagle can make its nest measuring 2.9 m wide and 6 m deep.

■ ■

6. SURPRISING PLANT KINGDOM

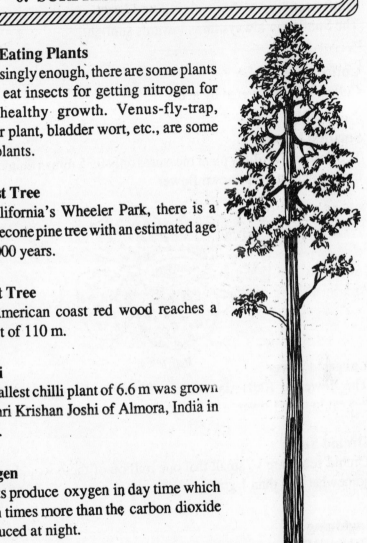

Meat Eating Plants
Surprisingly enough, there are some plants which eat insects for getting nitrogen for their healthy growth. Venus-fly-trap, pitcher plant, bladder wort, etc., are some such plants.

Oldest Tree
In California's Wheeler Park, there is a Bristlecone pine tree with an estimated age of 5,000 years.

Giant Tree
An American coast red wood reaches a height of 110 m.

Chilli
The tallest chilli plant of 6.6 m was grown by Shri Krishan Joshi of Almora, India in 1981.

Oxygen
Plants produce oxygen in day time which is ten times more than the carbon dioxide produced at night.

Bamboo
Bamboo is not a tree but a grass. It grows amazingly fast, at the rate of three feet a day.

Sunflower

Sun Flower.

The Sunflower always turns towards sunlight.

Coffee

Coffee was discovered by goats.

Smallest Flower

The flower of artillery plant measures only 0.35 mm in diameter. It is the smallest ever known flower.

Largest Flower

Rafflesia.

The flower of Rafflesia measures 90 cm in diameter and is the largest known flower.

Orchid Seeds

Orchid seeds are so small that one million of these would weigh somewhat less than 1 gm.

Lightning

Oaks and Poplars are struck by lightning more frequently than any other trees in England.

Boxwood

Boxwood is so heavy that it does not float on water but sinks.

Medicinal Plants
Numerous plant species produce drugs which are invaluable in modern medicine. The *foxglove* is the source of the drug digitals, which is used to treat heart disease.

Potato
A single potato can produce six or more new potatoes.

Seaweed
Seaweed is used in the manufacture of fertilizers, medicines, paint, toothpaste and in ice creams also.

Life
Life has been detected up to the heights of 8,230 m and up to the depths of 10,900 m.

Cactus
A cactus plant, only three feet tall may have roots spreading out to a length of ten feet across the desert.

Time Capsule
The oldest known living seed came from a North American Arctic Lupin. It was found in 1954, buried in frozen silt near Miller Greek in central Yukon-Canada, by a mining engineer named Schmidt. It had been there for 10,000 years. Yet, when scientists planted it, a plant grew which was identical to the modern plant.

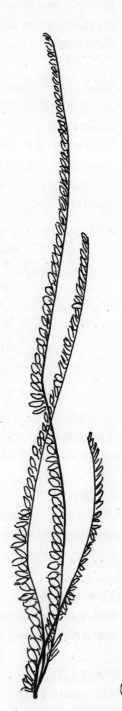

Talking Trees

In 1982, two American scientists made a startling claim that trees do appear to be able to communicate with each other specially of their kind.

Rise of the Rose

More than 8000 varieties of Rose have been developed for gardens, cultivation—yet all of them have descended from a mere handful of wild species. Until the end of 18th century, only four or five species were grown. They included the dog rose, misk rose, phoenician rose and the red province rose. Modern varieties such as hybrid tea roses and floribundas began to be grown only around 1900.

Rose Flowers.

Wheat

Wheat is being grown for the last 5,000 years. It was cultivated by farmers in the Middle East around 800 B.C.

Chillies

Chillies are hot due to the presence of about 0.1% of a chemical capsicum in the fruit. Chillies are native of America, but the largest crops by far are now grown in India.

Tree Trunk

The trunk of the baobab tree in Kenya is so long that some people make their homes with the hollowed out trunks.

Plant Life

(62) The greatest depth at which plant life has been found is 884 feet.

Potato
There are about 252 varieties of potato grown in the world.

Forest
Coniferous forests of the Northern USSR are the largest in the world.

Watermelon
A water melon weighing 90.7 kg was grown by Grace Garden in April 1980 at Arkansas, USA.

Mango
More than 1,000 varieties of mangoes are grown in the world of which about 550 were shown in the International Mango Festival in New Delhi in July 1991.

Mango.

Pineapple
H. Retiet of Malindi, Kenya, picked a pineapple in December 1978, whose weight was 17 pounds.

Mushroom
Edible mushrooms grow to their full size within seven days.

Flowers like Bird
Orange and blue flowers of the bird of paradise look like the feathers of a brightly coloured bird.

7. FACTS ABOUT PEOPLE

Monk

A Greek monk Mihallo Toltos never saw a woman in his life. When he was born, his mother died and the baby was taken the following day to a monastery atop the Mount Athos. He spent his life among the monks-isolated from women. Even female animals were not allowed to enter the monastery.

Cleopatra

Cleopatra always wore a fake beard when presiding over court proceedings.

Royal Role

Yu Brynner played the same role 4625 times. It was that of the king of Siam in the musical film, "The King and I."

Inspired by a Spider

King Robert Bruce after a defeat in AD 1306 took shelter in a cave. There, he saw a spider which tried six times to reach its web, but failed. Only after trying once more the spider succeeded. Witnessing this, Bruce resolved to fight once more and at this time he succeeded and became the master of Scotland.

Age
Shigechiyo Izume of Japan lived a life of 120 years and 237 days. He was born on 29th June 1865 and died on 21 Feb. 1986.

Fast
Angus Barbieri of Tayport, Fife remained on fasting for 382 days. During this period, he took only tea, coffee, water and sodawater.

Statesman and Inventor
Benjamin Franklin was a famous American Statesman besides being an inventor. He discovered atmospheric electricity by sheer accident.

Human Computer
The 13th root of a 100 digit number was extracted by Willem Klein of Netherlands just in 1 min. 28.8 sec. on April 7, 1981.

Longevity
Recorded longevity of man has been 120 years, while that of a tortoise is over 152 years.

Longest Marriage
The longest marriage of the world lasted for 86 years. Lady and Sir Nariman of India lived a happy married life for 86 years.

Choking Deaths
Every year about 3,000 Americans die by choking on food, 120 die in their bath tubs and 43,000 die in road accidents.

First Woman Ruler of Delhi
Razia Sultana was the first Woman ruler of Delhi, under the Mughal dynasty.

Mount Everest Woman Climber
Bachendri Pal was the first Indian woman to scale the Mount Everest.

Dada Saheb Award
Cine actress of yester years, Devika Rani was the first Indian woman to receive Dada Saheb Phalke Award.

Births
Mrs. Geraldine Brodrick gave birth to 9 children (5 male and 4 female) at Royal Hospital, Sydney, Australia on 13 June 1971.

Picasso.

Picasso
Picasso, the most prolific painter produced 13,500 paintings, 100,000 prints or engravings, 34,000 book illustrations and 300 sculptures and ceramics.

Deaths
About 10 million people die every year in the world.

Births
About 27 million children are born in the world every year.

Divorce
About 46.5% of world divorces takes place in USA every year.

Song
The most frequently sung song is, 'Happy Birthday to You'.

Recording
Miss Lata Mangeshker has sung about 30,000 solo, duet and chorus in 20 Indian Languages between 1948 to 1985.

Film Role
Jan Leighton of USA has played roles 3,350 times in films and television spots from 1951 to 1985.

Voting
In India, voting age is 18 years; but a person of 15 years of age can vote in Philippines.

Murder Rate
Maldives had almost no murder so far, while Brazil has the highest.

Omelette

In Hotel Le Meridien, Vancouver-Canada, an Omelette of 45,000 eggs was cooked on 27th Jan. 1986.

Famine

About 3 crore people died in Northern China in the famine from 1959 to 1961.

Milking

Andy Faust at Collinsville, Oklahoma USA in 1937 milked 120 gallons of milk in 12 hours.

Longest Moustache

Pt. Masuriya Din of Pratapgarh district (U.P.) had moustache 259 cm long in 1962.

Pt. Masuriya Din.

Blood Donor

Allen Doster of USA donated 851.76 litre of blood from 1966 to 1986.

Nails

Shridhar Chilal of Pune (India) had allowed his 5 nails of left hand to grow to a length of 363.2 cm.

Iron Lung

Mrs. Laurel Nisbel of USA survived for 37 years and 58 days on lungs made of metal iron.

Richard

Richard the Lion-hearted King of England spent more than 95 per cent of his reign away from his kingdom and visited England only twice.

Italian Flag

Italian Flag was designed by Napoleon Bonaparte.

Napoleon Bonaparte

Husband's Name

Women of the Asin Kirghiz tribe face instant divorce, if they dare to mention their husband's names.

I.Q.

If you have on IQ of 180 or more you are literally one person in a million.

Big Ben

Benjamin Hall, the 18th Century Politician weighed some 158 kg which explains why the bell named after him is called Big Ben.

Belief

In India, the Chenchu tribe believe that sex at night produces blind children.

Tottoo

Rustly Field is the world's most tattooed lady. Her husband has spent more than 20 years in decorating the body with more than 2,500 designs.

Man's Existence
Though life began on Earth some 3.5 billion years ago, Man has existed only for the last one million years.

Policemen
American policemen are known as 'Cops' while those of London as 'Bobbies'.

Pilots
Pilots salute each other, by tilting or dipping their plane's wings.

Tattoo's Clothing
Tattoo designs once took the place of clothing for some Japanese people, who completely covered themselves with tattoos from head to toe.

Garmets
A woman of the Toda tribe of Southern India gets only two garments in her life time, one during her childhood and the second when she gets married.

America's Presidents
Four of America's 39 Presidents have died at the hands of assassins. Abraham Lincoln was shot in Washington's theatre in 1865 by John Wilkes Booth. James Garfield was shot in 1881 by Charles Guiteau. William Mekinley was shot by Leon Czolyosz in 1901. John F. Kennedy was shot in 1963 by Lee Harvey Oswald.

Taj Mahal

Labour of Love
Twenty thousand men laboured for nearly 20 years to bring the Taj Mahal at Agra, to its final shining glory of perfection beside the Yamuna river. The building, a mausoleum of pure white marble, was built by the Mughal emperor Shah Jahan to house the body of his beloved second wife, Mumtaz Mahal.

Number of Children
Abdul Aziz, who in 1932 became the first king of what is now the Saudi Arabia, had at least 79 children.

Human Baby — a Wolf Child
Children left in the wild or otherwise deprived of fellow human beings due to circumstances beyond one's control do not learn how to speak spontaneously. There are more than '50 recorded cases' of 'wolf children' who have been found living among animals. All were mentally retarded and unable to speak.

Explorer Who Bought a Wife
The Victorian explorer, Samuel Baker, made a most unusual purchase: he bought himself a wife. She was a Hungarian girl whom Baker, a widower, rescued from Turkish slavery at a slave auction.

Half a Billion in a Day
The eccentric American Recluse Howard Hughes (1905-76) once made half a billion dollars in one day. He received a single banker's draft for $546,549,771 in 1966 in return for his 75 per cent holding in Trans World Airlines.

Deepest Hole of Earth

The world's deepest borehole is an exploratoy geological drilling in the Kola Peninsula, in northern Russia. In 1984, it was more than four-fifths of the way to its target depth of 15,000 m.

Super Highway in the Sky

Streches of the Great Royal Road, a 4800 km (3000 mile) super highway built by the Incas, are still visible along the Andes of South America. It was constructed between about AD 1200 and the coming of the Spanish in the 16th Century. The road was about 23 ft. wide, and was marked on each side by a low stone wall.

From the Beginning till Now

The oldest man-made structures built in 3250 BC still standing are stone henge-like temples. The megalithic buildings are at Magarr and Skorba on Motta and a Ggantija on the nearby island of Gozo.

Precious Umbrella

A gilded and jewelled umbrella erected in AD 1871 crowns the 6th century Shwedagon pagoda in Burma. The eight fold path by Buddhism was presented by king Mindon. The pagoda, a solid brick spire is 99 m high. The spire is covered with 8688 thin laminated sheets of gold, each about 300 sq. mm. At modern prices, each of the golden sheets is worth about £ 5000.

Eskimo Health

Eskimos who eat more fat compared to others in the world hardly had any heart diseases.

And Two that Did

Two irrigation dams built by Roman Engineers in the 2nd century AD in Merida, Spain, are still in use. The only major maintenance work they have needed in the past 1800 years has been the renewal of their stone facings, carried out in the 1930s.

Product of a Garden Shed

The American Henry Ford, founder of the Ford Motor Company, made his first car in the garden shed at his home in Michigan in 1896.

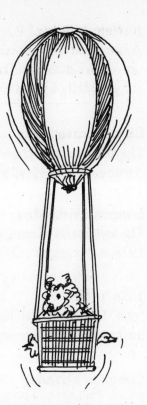

First Air Transport

The first living creatures to be transported by air were a sheep, a cock and a duck. The French Montgdfier brothers – whose hot air balloon made the first manned flight in Novermber 1783 – sent the animals from Versailles under a balloon in September the same year, to see if they would be harmed by the thin air. They survived unharmed except the damage to one of the wings of the cock, probably by a kick from the sheep.

Fatal Kiss

A Chinese Poet, Li Po is said to have drowned after leaving out of a boat in a drunken attempt to kiss reflection of the moon, on sea water.

Flea Catch

In 1928, a Chinese caught 21,000 fleas in four hours.

Buffalo Milking

Among the Toda tribe of Nilgiri—Ootacamund in Tamil Nadu, only men can milk buffaloes, women cannot. Milk must be churned for ghee only by a priest in the temple precincts.

Blow from the Blue

The only person known to have been hit by a meteorite is an American, Mrs. Hewlett Hodges.

Longest Lived Man

The longest lived man was Shirali Nislimov who died on Sept. 8, 1978 at the age of 168 years.

John Tyler

John Tyler was on his knees playing marbles, when he was informed that he has become US President in 1842.

Common Birthday

Prince Charles and Pt. Jawahar Lal Nehru have a common birthday of 14th November every year.

Prince Charles and Pt. Nehru.

Rice Eaters
More than 2.5 billion people of the world (more than half of the world's people) are rice eaters.

Bath
People did not believe in taking baths in Elizabethan times, because they thought water removed the natural oil from their skins and allowed diseases causing bacteria to enter the body through the skin.

Age
The number of people over 63 years of age in the world are 300 million. This became 370 million by the year AD 2000 and will become 465 million by the year AD 2200.

Helen
Helen, Greek wife of Chandragupta Maurya of Magadha introduced Saree as a costume for women in India.

Glass House
Philip Johnson constructed a house at New Canaan, Connecticut, purely on glass. It is rectangular in shape and has thin columns of steel to support its roof.

Paper House
Elis F. Stenman made a paper house in Massachusetts by using 100,000 newspapers. The walls of this house were made of layers of pasted and folded newspapers. Papers rolled into different sizes make up the furniture which includes tables, chairs and lamp shades. Its construction was completed in 1942.

House of Bottles

A house of bottles was made by George Plumb of Canada in 1978. The entire house is constructed of 18,000 liquor, soda, medicine and beer bottles.

Cricketer

The legendary English Cricketer, Dr. W.G. Grace began playing at the age of nine and continued until he was 61.

Paavo Nurmi

Paavo Nurmi of Finland was a cart puller. He became a famous runner. He won 12 medals (nine gold and three silver) in the Olympic games of 1920, 1924 and 1928.

Olympic Gold Medal

Both King Constantine of Greece and king Olav of Norway won Olympic gold medals for sailing.

Gold Medals

The world record seven gold medals, won at the 1972 Munich Olympic Games by American swimmer Mark Spitz, are worth little as bullion.

Carl Lewis

Carl Lewis, the star athlete from USA could leap over twelve people shoulder to shoulder.

Muhammad Ali

Famous boxer Muhammad Ali earned largest fortune of about 60 million dollars from October 1960 to August 1979 in 59 fights comprising 529 rounds.

Muhammad Ali.

Edward Jenner

The small pox vaccination was discovered by Edward Jenner by taking some fluid from the finger of a dairy maid who was suffering from cow pox.

Noureddin Kiannouri

In 1983, Ayatollah Khomeini, the spiritual leader of Iran suddenly dissolved the Tudeh party following the secretary general Noureddin Kiannouri's involvement with KGB.

Bull Killer

Rafael Molina known as Lagartijo, the famous 19th century bull-fighter, killed some 4867 bulls.

Archimedes

Archimedes, the famous scientist, was killed by a Roman soldier.

W.K. Roentgen

Roentgen, just after discovering the X-rays took the first photograph of his wife's hand.

John F. Kennedy

The 35th US President John F. Kennedy (1917-1963) in December 1961 spoke with a recorded speed of 327 words per minute in a public meeting.

Leonardo da Vinci.

Ten Men in One
Leonardo da Vinci has been known as ten men in one because he was a painter, inventor, lute player, sculptor, military engineer, scientific observer, anatomist, architect, town planner as well as a committed designer.

Solution in a Dream
Kekule got the solution to benzene molecular structure in a dream.

Alfred Nobel
Inventor of the most disastrous explosive dynamite constituted the Nobel Prize from the earnings of dynamite.

H.J. Bhabha
Famous Nuclear physicist H.J. Bhabha of India died in a plane crash in 1966.

Words and Sentences
Some of the World's most lasting literary works—including fiction, autobiography, poetry and philosophy—were written or attempted to begin while their authors were in prison.

Rajiv Gandhi.

Rajiv Gandhi

In the election held on 24th December, 1984 for the Indian lower house of Parliament, Rajiv Gandhi came with a thumping majority securing 405 seats in a house of 542 for his Congress-I political party.

■ ■

Washington D.C.
D.C. in Washington D.C. stands for District of Columbia.

Land of the Midnight Sun — Norway.

Norway
Norway is called the land of midnight sun because sun does not set from May till the fall of July.

Airport
International Airport at Chicago is so busy that on an average about 85 aeroplanes land and take-off from this airport every hour.

Land of Lakes
There are 60,000 lakes in Finland and it is known as the 'Land of Lakes'.

Sudan
Sudan in Africa is surrounded by eight countries — Egypt, Libya, Chad, Central African Republic, Zaire, Uganda, Kenya and Ethiopia.

Orange River

The orange river in South Africa is considered richest because it carries diamonds as it flows.

Italy.

Italy

Italy is in the shape of a boat.

Winter

The winter of 1925 was so cold in Canada that the Niagara Falls were completely frozen.

Holland Port

Rotterdam in Holland is the largest port and it handles three million tonnes of cargo every year.

Chinese Capital

The Chinese capital Beijing having a population of 10 million people has only 1800 cars.

Tea Currency

Solid blocks of tea were used as currency in Siberia until the 19th century.

Hole in the Earth

If a hole was dug straight through the Earth from Shanghai, it would come out on the other side of the globe very near Buenos Aires.

Fridge

Eskimos use fridge to prevent their food from freezing.

Egyptian
The Egyptians used the annual flooding of the Nile river to accurately set up their calendar.

Vatican City
The smallest independent country in the world is Vatican city with a zero birth rate. It has a population of barely 800 people.

Countries
There are 229 countries in the world of which 170 are sovereign and 59 non-sovereign.

House Numbering
Houses were first numbered in Paris in 1463. The practice was adopted in London some 300 years later.

Tokyo
The ancient name of Tokyo is Edo.

Pain
Spain is always in pain.

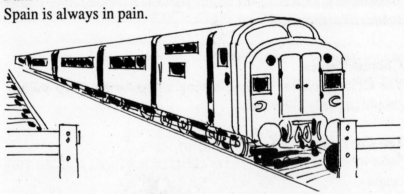

First Electric Train in India
The first electric train in India ran between V.T. (Bombay) an Kurla in 1925.

Cash Collection
The daily cash collection at the famous Tirupati Temple in Andhra Pradesh is Rs. 10 lakhs.

Cold

At places of the lowest temperature like Siberia, people do not infect with cold because it is too cold for the bacteria to grow.

Big Hole

The world's largest man-made hole is at Kimberley, South Africa. It has a perimeter of 1.6 km and 800 m deep. It was dug in 1871 for obtaining diamonds. It yielded so far three tonnes of diamonds.

Earth Quakes

Japan has, an average, 1000 noticeable earthquakes every year.

Bermuda Triangle

Bermuda Triangle or Devils triangle is part of the North Atlantic Ocean, roughly between Florida, Bermuda and the Sargasso sea. It is so dangerous that a number of aircraft and ships have vanished there.

Worst Floods

More than 200 million people of China were badly affected by floods during July 1991.

Population

The present population of 5 billion plus people of the world will become 15 billion by 2080.

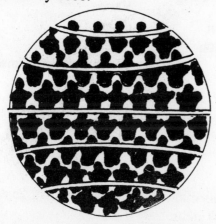

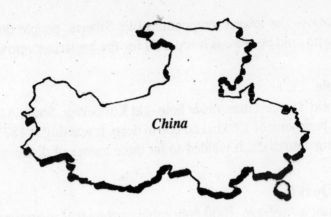

China

Population

About 40 per cent of world population lives in China and India.

Russia

Rusia is the largest country in land mass.

Biggest Structure	: Great Wall of China
Tallest Skyscraper	: Sears Tower in Chicago-443 m high
Highest Dam	: Under construction in Russia
Longest Tunnel	: Japan-54 km long
Most Populous City	: Maxico City
Highest Capital	: La Paz, Bolivia
Highest City	: Lhasa
Most Expensive City to live	: Tokyo, Japan
Widest Waterfall	: Khone
Largest Population	: China
Smallest Population	: Vatican City
Largest Park	: Wood Buffalo, Canada.

9. WONDERS OF SCIENCE & TECHNOLOGY

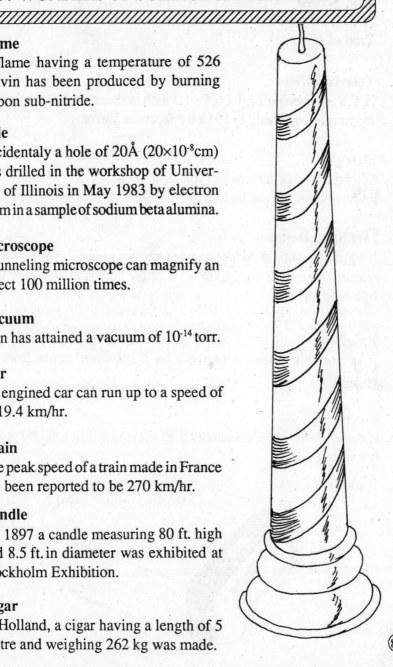

Flame
A flame having a temperature of 526 Kelvin has been produced by burning carbon sub-nitride.

Hole
Accidentaly a hole of 20Å (20×10⁻⁸cm) was drilled in the workshop of University of Illinois in May 1983 by electron beam in a sample of sodium beta alumina.

Microscope
A tunneling microscope can magnify an object 100 million times.

Vacuum
Man has attained a vacuum of 10^{-14} torr.

Car
Jet engined car can run up to a speed of 1019.4 km/hr.

Train
The peak speed of a train made in France has been reported to be 270 km/hr.

Candle
In 1897 a candle measuring 80 ft. high and 8.5 ft. in diameter was exhibited at Stockholm Exhibition.

Cigar
In Holland, a cigar having a length of 5 metre and weighing 262 kg was made.

Radio Set
The smallest radio set 9 × 5.4 × 1.3 cm. has been made by Toshiba Japan.

T.V. Screen
A T.V. screen 80 ft. × 150 ft. was made in 1985 by Sony Jumbo Tron of Japan.

Television Set
A T.V. set measuring 3 × 6.5 × 1.5 inch in size and about one pound by weight was made in 1985 by Japanese Epson.

Energy
Scientists today can convert matter into energy. Surprisingly, one gram of uranium produces same energy as 30,000 g. of coal.

Lightning Danger
If your hair should suddenly stand end-on phase for no apparent reason, there is a strong likelihood of the person to be struck by a lightning stroke.

Rainbow
It is possible to see a rainbow as a complete circle from an aeroplane.

Electric Shaver
Electric shaver uses less energy than shaving with a hand razor and hot water.

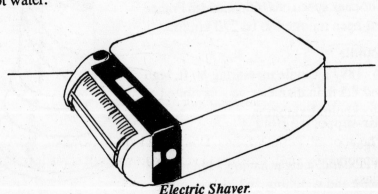

Electric Shaver.

Vinegar
A litre of vinegar is heavier in winter than in summer.

Reading Machine
US scientists have developed a computerised machine which can read any written document just like human beings.

Wonder Bricks
Scientists have developed polyurethane bricks which float on water. They are stronger than conventional mud-bricks.

Space Shuttle·
Space shuttle is a strange spacecraft which can land on Earth like an aeroplane.

Fermentation
A barrel of juice or wine would take about a year or two to ferment naturally into vinegar.

Swimming
It is easier to swim in a sea rather to a river because the density of sea water is more compared to that of river water due to dissolved salts.

Swimming in Sea is Easier.

Air-supported Roof
The roof of Portaik Silver Dome Stadium, Michigan, USA, is supported by air. It does not have support walls. It is made of fibre glass.

Feather-light Shoes.

Feather-footed
Feather-light shoes created by New York designer Yanturni in 1920s took some three years to make, and he refused even to make these without a $ 1,000 deposit.

Ambulance
Ambulances were developed by Napoleon's surgeon in his Italian company of 1796-97.

The Impossible Typewriter
The Japanese, whose genius values for machines brought them in the forefront of the industrial world, have yet not mastered the humble typewriter. The reason behind is that even the every day language requires more than 2000 characters far more than would fit on to a conventional keyboard.

The World's Most Expensive Water
The world's most expensive water is heavy water used as moderator in nuclear reactors. It costs more than £ 200 per litre.

Cooling Off
The refrigerating plant with the cooling capacity of 2,500 tonnes of ice is installed in the world's deepest mine: the Western Deep levels Gold mine at Carletonville, South Africa. Without the cooling plant, the temperature at the lowest levels 3777 m down would be as high as 55°C.

A Suspension Bridge.

Humber Highway

The new Humber Bridge in northern England—currently the world's longest suspension bridge—has a deck with a curved underside, like an upside-down aeroplane wing, so that the stronger the wind the more firmly it holds itself in place. In order to damp down vibrations at low wind speeds the cables that hold the roadway, are set at an angle. The bridges's central span is 1,410 m long and the towers are so apart that they are 36 mm out of parallel to allow for the curvature of the Earth.

Super Computers

The speed at which a super computer works is astonishing. The fastest was capable of 1,300 million computations per second. The new super computers will be capable of more than 10,000 million calculation per second.

Safety Pin

The safety pin was invented by New York's Walter Hunt in 1849. It took him three hours to design it to raise the money to pay a seven pound debt.

TV Sets

China has more than 65 million TV sets. A good programme in this country is watched by more than 325 million people — the largest television audience across the world.

Requiem for a Cow
In November 1960, an American rocket launched from Cape Canaveral, Florida, went off the course and crushed in Cuba, killing a cow. The Cuban government gave the cow an official funeral, as the victim of imperialist aggression.

Number of Molecules
A drop of water contains 15,000,000,000, 000,000,000,000 number of molecules.

NMR
Nuclear Magnetic Resonance scanner can locate the tumours in the body as small as 1 mm in diameter.

Dangerous Chemical
TCDD is a man-made chemical which is 150,000 times more deadly than cyanide.

A Wonder Camera
A camera for fusion research at Essex University, England, is so fast that it can register images at a rate of 3000 million per sec.

Copper
(90) Copper turns green when exposed to air for a pretty long time.

Temperature
At Princeton Plasma Physics Laboratory, USA, a scientist has produced successfully a temperature of 82 million degree centigrade.

Space Telescope
A very large telescope is revolving around the earth in space to observe peculiarities of space.

Space Telescope.

Thermometer
Man has made an extremely small thermometer which can measure the temperature of a single living cell. Its tip is one micron in diameter.

Nitrous Oxide
Nitrous oxide gas can make you laugh. That is why it is called laughing gas.

Leap Year
Julius Caesar introduced the leap year in the Gregarian calendar.

Saccharin
Saccharin is 500 to 700 times more sweeter than sugar.

Word Without Vowel
RHYTHM is a six letter word which has no vowel.

Perfumes
Sperm whale produces ambergris which is used for making perfumes.

Test Tube Baby
The world's first baby conceived in a test tube outside the mother's body was born in Oldham, England. Her name is Louise Joy Brown.

Number of Cells
There are more than 26 billion cells in a new born baby.

Bacteria
Bacteria had been discovered at an altitude of 1,35,000 ft, during a space flight in April 1967.

Lightest Gas	: Hydrogen
Heaviest Metal	: Osmium
Lightest Metal	: Lithium
Hardest Substance	: Diamond
Smallest Unit of Length	: Attometre

Jet Plane
A jet plane can fly around the Earth in less than a day.

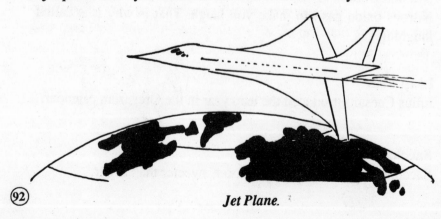

Jet Plane.

Long Distance
In 1974, a radio message from Earth was beamed towards a star cluster called M-13 in the constellation of Hercules. If this message gets back to Earth, it will not be received here before the year 50,000 A.D.

Lead
There is no lead in a lead pencil, it consists of non-metal graphite.

Diamond
Diamond is an allotrope of Carbon.

Dry Ice
Solid carbon dioxide is called dry ice, because when it melts it does not change into liquid but vapourises directly.

Quantity of Salt
If salt of all the oceans is collected and dried, one can make a wall 288 kms high and 1.6 km thick around the perimeter of the Earth along the equator.

Number of Molecules
One litre of air contains 30,000 million, million, million molecules.

Ball Game
If two balls of the same size, one of rubber and the other of steel, are thrown with equal force on a pavement, then the steel ball will bounce higher.

Ball Game.

Edison.

Thomas Alva Edison

Thomas Alva Edison, the wizard of Menlo Park, produced more than 1,000 inventions during his lifetime.

Atomic Clock

During the last two decades, scientists have developed an extremely accurate clock known as atomic clock, which remains accurate to one second over a period of 1,700,000 years.

Smaller Than Small

Most people think electron as the smallest particle but it is not true. Much smaller than electron is photon. Its mass is about 3×10^{-50} grams.

Magic Mirror

Magic mirrors have been made in China and Japan for centuries. If you look into one of these highly polished bronze mirrors, you see only your face; but, if you hold the mirror towards the sun and reflect the light on to a white surface, the reflection shows a design, such as the picture of Buddha.

Heaviest and Lightest

Lithium is the lightest metal while Osmium is the densest metal. A two feet by two feet by two feet slab of Osmium weighs equivalent to an elephant.

Ice

Ice does not melt when kept in liquid ammonia.

Quick Silver
Quick silver is not silver, but it is another name of mercury melt which is the only liquid metal. It is so heavy that a piece of iron floats on its surface.

Lie Detector
Lie detector or polygraph is a wonder machine that can detect the lies told by criminals.

Laser Beams
Laser beams are so powerful that they can drill hole in diamond, the hardest substance.

Fastest Car
The Porsche 9591, has a top road tested speed of 317 km/hr which is highest so far.

Fool's Gold
Many early prospectors mistook iron pyrites — a gold coloured iron ore — for gold. The ore became known as fool's gold.

Asbestos
Asbestos is a fire resistant material which does not burn even up to 3,000°C.

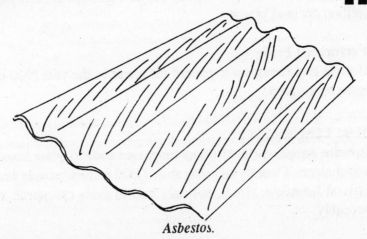

Asbestos.

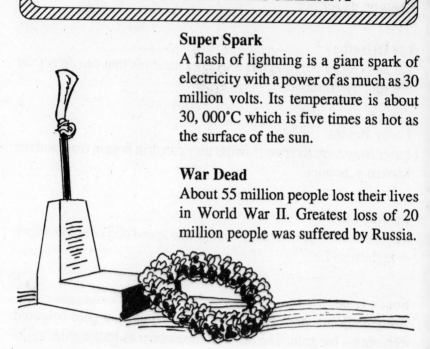

Super Spark

A flash of lightning is a giant spark of electricity with a power of as much as 30 million volts. Its temperature is about 30, 000°C which is five times as hot as the surface of the sun.

War Dead

About 55 million people lost their lives in World War II. Greatest loss of 20 million people was suffered by Russia.

Without End

Pi is a number (ratio of the circumference of a circle to its diameter) that can never be absolutely calculated. Its approximate value is taken as 22/7 = 3.14. A computer has calculated *pi* to more than 16 million decimal places.

Perforated Pride

Bolivia and Paraguay triggered off a war in the year 1930 on the issue of a stamp.

Most Languages

In India, people speak 15 major languages and 857 other languages and dialects. Country of more than 1,000 million people has one official language, Hindi, but only half of them can speak it im–peccably.

Finger Prints
Finger prints of any two persons in the world are not exactly the same. This fact is used to identify criminals.

Talcum Powder
Perfumed talcum powder is made from a mineral called Talc. It is the softest possible mineral known to man.

Book without E
The book *Gadby* written by Earnest Wright in 1939 is a 50,000 word book. It does not contain a single word with an 'E' in it.

T.V. Programme
The royal wedding of Britain's prince of Wales and Lady Diana Spencer in 1981 was seen by 750 million viewers on T.V.

Malaria
Every year more than 40 million people suffer from malaria owing to mosquito bites.

Diagnosis by Nose
Before the modern medicine, European Doctors diagnosed-patients by their nose.

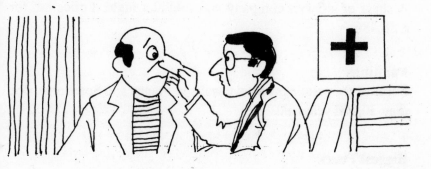

Alphabet

Combodian language has some 72 alphabet, compared to other languages.

Longest Word

The longest regularly formed English word is *Praetertranssubstantiationalistically* which contains 37 letters.

Star Trek

Start Trek has been the most expensive film.

Pastry

A pastry of 1607 ft. 2 inch long was made on 15 June 1983 by the Gothenburg Patissiers Association of Sweden.

Pencils

There are 350 different kinds of pencils manufactured today with more than 2 billion sold each year in the United States alone.

Share

A share of a Swiss company was sold at a highest price i.e., for $ 38,486.

Paintings

Some of the paintings on cave walls in France and Spain are more than 30,000 years old.

Biggest Pearl

One famous pearl - *the Hope pearl* - was a *baroque* weighing about 300 gms.

Buttons
Although, today buttons are made of plastic, sheels, glass, metal etc., the ancient Greeks, some 4000 years ago had buttons made out of solid gold.

Tip
The word **'tip'** is an abbreviation of **'To Insure Promptness'**

English Word from the Name of Greek Goddess
The English word for cleanliness — hygiene, comes from the name of a Greek goddess of health, *Hygieia.*

The living goddess
Hindus in Nepal worship a living goddess — a young girl — known as *Kumari Devi,* a title meaning *'Living Goddess'.* She is chosen from Buddhist goldsmith's caste when she is three years old and must be without any physical blemish. She assumes divinity after proving her bravery by remaining alone for a while in a room filled with skeletons and gruesome objects.

Two-in-one
The flag of Paraguay is the only national flag which is not the same on both sides. One side features red, white and blue stripes with the national arms on white stripe. The other has the same stripes - but with the treasury seal upon the white one.

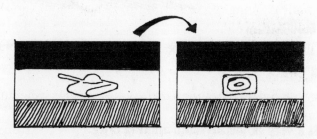

The Sum that's Always the Same

Take any three figure number in which the first figure is larger than the last, say 521. Reverse it, making 125 and subtract the smaller from the larger, making 396. Now add the result to the same number reversed, 693. The answer is 1089, and will be 1089 whatever number you start with.

Counting, Counting

If a person counts at the rate of 100 numbers a minute, and kept on counting for eight hours a day, five days a week, it would take a little over four weeks to count to 1 million and just over 80 years to reach 1000 million, or what is now often called one billion.

Breads

More than 200 varieties of bread are produced in Germany.

Mouse with Million Fans

Walt Disney's most popular cartoon figure Mickey Mouse had largest possible number of fans. Mickey received 800,000 letters from the fans at an average of more than 2,000 a day.

Chip Revolution

More than 64,000 bytes can be stored on a single finger nail sized silicon chip.

LSD

LSD is a very powerful hallucinating drug.

Nobel Prizes

There have been only three persons in the world namely Madam Curie, John Bardeen and Linus Pauling, each one of them received Nobel Prize twice in their lifetime. No other family except Curie has won five Nobel Prizes.

A Taxi.

Taxi Colour

The standard yellow and black colour of Taxis have originated from the black and yellow uniform worn for the first time by the cab drivers of London on August 13, 1897.

All the World's Gold

The total amount of gold produced since the stone age is estimated to be about 100,000 tonnes and about half of this has been mined since 1850.

Leap Year

A *leap year* is a multiple of four, however, years ending in *zero zero* which are not divisible by 400 form an exception to it. For example 1700 and 1800, though divisible by four, are not leap years.

First Atom Bomb

The first atom bomb, developed under the supervision of Oppenheimer, was tested on July 16, 1945.

Disease Control

About 18 diseases can be prevented by vaccination.

Eggs
Peter Dowdeswell ate 14 boiled eggs in 58 seconds.

Nuclear Weapons
Stockpile of Nuclear weapons in the world is roughly equivalent to 15 thousand mega tonnes of TNT. If distributed to the people of the world, each one will get three tones of TNT.

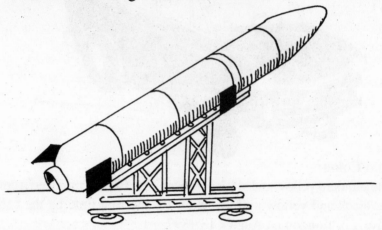

Gravitation
Idea of gravitation came to Newton by seeing an apple falling from the tree.

Radio Stations
USA has 9,512 radio stations, which is the largest number in the world.

Expo-70
Expo-70 at Osaka, Japan was seen by 64,218,770 people from all over the world.

Door
We have seen many large sized doors, but there is one in vehicle As Assembly building near Cape Canaveral, Florida which is 460 ft high.

Diamonds from a Volcano

Volcanic Mount Pinatubo, Philippines was dormant for the last 600 years. It became erupting on June 9,1991. Amazingly this time the volcanic ash contained crystals like diamonds. These were collected by the children and a matchboxful was sold to local businessmen at 200 pesos (7 dollars).

Traditional harem for a Boy

No other pharaoh of Egypt can compare with Ramesses II for achievement and self-glorification. He was an army captain at the age of ten and had his traditional harem.

Dance

Will Kemp Morris in 1599 danced his way from London to Norwiche in 9 days.

Bananas

Bananas
Dr. Ronald L. Alkana of California, Irvine ate 17 bananas in 2 minutes on 7 December 1973.

■ ■

PRACTICAL PALMISTRY

80/-

emy size, pp: 365
so available in Hindi

Palmistry for Beginners

Discover the mysteries of Palmistry

88/-

Demy size, pp: 282

Palmistry of Romance

Love's Paradise

80/-

Demy size, pp: 180

Marriage-Matching Astrologically

80/-

Demy size, pp: 142

Astrology for Layman

80/-

Demy size, pp: 184

Explore the Astrology

New

96/-

Demy size, pp: 200

LAL KITAB

A Rare Book On Astrology

195/-

size, pp: 336
ardbound)

INSTANT HAND WRITING ANALYSIS

A Key to Personal Success

RUTH GARDNER

80/-

Demy size, pp: 152

THE PROPHECIES OF NOSTRADAMUS

60/-

Demy size, pp: 160

Healing Power of GEMS AND STONES

80/-

Demy size, pp: 136

Fascinating world of DREAMS

And what they mean to you

60/-

Demy size, pp: 144

PRACTICAL HYPNOTISM

75/-

Demy size, pp: 236
Also available in Hindi

ADVANCED HYPNOTISM

120/-

Big size, pp: 264

Hypnotism for Beginners

Easy techniques to practise hypnotism

68/-

Demy size, pp: 160

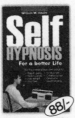

Self HYPNOSIS

For a better Life

88/-

Demy size, pp: 184

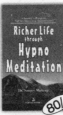

Richer Life through Hypno Meditation

80/-

Demy size, pp: 107

NUMEROLOGY

A Complete Guide to Understanding and Using Your Numbers of Destiny

KEY TO YOUR INNER SELF

88/-

Demy size, pp: 272

Numerology of Romance

Love by Numbers

80/-

Demy size, pp: 222

Horoscope Reading

135/-

Big size, pp: 248

PREDICTIONS FOR A NEW MILLENNIUM

1996 to 2012

88/-

Demy size, pp: 272

Benefits of Vaastu & Feng Shui

80/-

Demy size, pp: 144

CHAKRA & KUNDALINI WORKBOOK

110/-

Demy size, pp: 264

Vaastu

Sorrections without Demolition

60/-

Demy size, pp: 92

Numerology

Know your Lucky Numbers for every sphere of life

68/-

Demy size, pp: 120

BODY Language

80/-

Demy size, pp: 120
(Also available in Hindi)

SELF-IMPROVEMENT

Demy size, pp: 160
Also available in Hindi
and Bangla

Demy size, pp: 136
Also available in Hindi

Demy size, pp: 64
Also available in Hindi

Demy size, pp: 80
Also available in Hindi

Demy size, pp: 156

Demy size, pp: 290

Demy size, pp: 184

Demy size, pp: 192

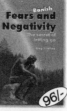
Demy size, pp: 240

Demy size, pp: 240

Demy size, pp: 304

Demy size, pp: 180

Demy size, pp: 128

Demy size, pp: 218

Demy size, pp: 174

Demy size, pp: 176

Demy size, pp: 140

Demy size, pp: 140

Demy size, pp: 155

Demy size, pp: 128

Demy size, pp: 176

Demy size, pp: 176

Demy size, pp: 136

Demy size, pp: 176

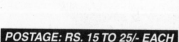

POSTAGE: RS. 15 TO 25/- EACH

4

Demy size, pp: 96

Demy size, pp: 176

Big size, pp: 168

SELF-IMPROVEMENT

 **31 Mantras for Personality Development**
60/-
Demy size, pp: 104

 **The Portrait of a Complete Man**
80/-
Demy size, pp: 176

 **The 4-Lane Expressway to STRESS MANAGEMENT**
95/-
Demy size, pp: 112

 **The Book of Etiquette and Manners**
68/-
Demy size, pp: 136

 **The Secrets of Marital Bliss**
80/-
Demy size, pp: 176

 **How to integrate the self**
80/-
Demy size, pp: 112

 **Thought-Provoking JOKES**
80/-
Demy size, pp: 176

 **The Portrait of a Perfect WOMAN**
80/-
Demy size, pp: 128

 **SECRETS OF HAPPINESS** — Tanushree Podder
80/-
Demy size, pp: 192

 **Hello! Just married or about to marry?**
80/-
Demy size, pp: 144

 **365 GEMS FOR HOLISTIC LIVING — A DAILY DOSE OF INSPIRATION** — ALAN COHEN
120/-
Demy size, pp: 376 (Hardbound)

 **The Art of Happy Living**
96/-
Demy size, pp: 168

 **freedom from thought**
96/-
Demy size, pp: 160

 **TALES OF WISDOM — Morale-building 57 Tales for Children**
60/-
Demy size, pp: 160

 **50 Moral Tales ...from The Gurukul**
68/-
Big size, pp: 160 (In 2 colour)

 **The Portrait of a Super Student**
80/-
Demy size, pp: 160 (In 2 colour)

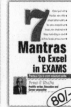 **7 Mantras to Excel in EXAMS**
80/-
Demy size, pp: 160

 **Boost Your Brain-Power** — Dr G Francis Xavier, PhD, The Great Motivator
96/-
Demy size, pp: 144

 **Immortal Sayings**
96/-
Demy size, pp: 192

 **2000 TITBITS & SATIRES — TO MAKE YOU GRIN, SMIRK & LAUGH**
68/-
Demy size, pp: 176

 **Notable Quotes & Noble Thoughts**
60/-
Demy size, pp: 96

 **A Treasury of Inspirational Thoughts**
68/-
Demy size, pp: 144

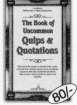 **The Book of Uncommon Quips & Quotations**
80/-
Demy size, pp: 128

 **The Book of COMMON & UNCOMMON PROVERBS**
96/-
Big size, pp: 128

 **The Complete Guide to MEMORY MASTERY — ORGANISING & DEVELOPING THE POWER OF YOUR MIND** — HARRY LORAYNE
60/-
Big size, pp: 312

POSTAGE: RS. 15 TO 25/- EACH

5

CAREER/STUDENT DEVELOPMENT/MANAGEMENT

Become a Successful SPEAKER — Don Aslett
68/-
Demy size, pp: 136

SUCCESS SECRETS — A COMMON-SENSE GUIDE TO LIFELONG ACHIEVEMENT
120/-
Demy size, pp: 256

Youngster's Guide for PERSONAL DEVELOPMENT
68/-
Demy size, pp: 120

100 You can Become Rich
80/-
Demy size, pp: 128

SMART MEMORY — Techniques to Improve Memory
68/-
Demy size, pp: 138

How to Motivate Others
8
Big size, pp: 1

SOLVE YOUR PROBLEMS — The Birbal Way
68/-
Demy size, pp: 200

TEENS TO TWENTIES — A guide for youngsters
68/-
Demy size, pp: 120

Create your own SUCCESS STORY & Live Life King-Size
80/-
Demy size, pp: 120

Making friends and doing business in Europe
96/-
Demy size, pp: 288

The Street Smart Salesman
88/-
Demy size, pp: 208

How to be a favourite with your BOSS
8
Big size, pp: 1

20 Keys for SUCCESS in JOB & CAREER
80/-
Demy size, pp: 144

GREAT SPEAKERS AREN'T BORN — The Complete Guide to Winning Presentations
88/-
Demy size, pp: 200

Skills for Excellence
88/-
Demy size, pp: 184

How to be the Complete Professional Salesperson — Robert L. Shook
120/-
Demy size, pp: 248

LET'S GET RESULTS NOT EXCUSES!
195/-
Big size, pp: 240

The Voyage to Excellence
3
Big size, pp: 2 — Hardbound

U.S. VISA MADE EASY — a practical guide
220/-
Big size, pp: 188

MARKETING WITH SPEECHES AND SEMINARS — Your Key to More Clients and Referrals
80/-
Demy size, pp: 176

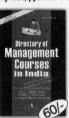
Directory of Management Courses in India
60/-
Demy size, pp: 392

BEGINNERS' GUIDE TO JOURNALISM
80/-
Demy size, pp: 128

Study & Immigration in USA
95/-
Demy size, pp: 128

MEDICAL TRANSCRIPTION
4
Big size, pp: 4

POSTAGE: RS. 15 TO 25/- EACH

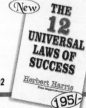
THE 12 UNIVERSAL LAWS OF SUCCESS — Herbert Harris
195/-
Demy size, pp: 192

6

Bite-sized bits on Common-sense Management

Gerard Assey

150/-

Big size, pp: 100

Mastering Salary Negotiations

How to skilfully negotiate the best remuneration package

96/-

Demy size, pp: 96

WINNING Résumé

80/-

Demy size, pp: 136

GROUP DISCUSSION For Admissions & Jobs

88/-

Demy size, pp: 200

Business Ideas you can turn into Cash

80/-

Demy size, pp: 128

Multiple Career Choices For Post-Graduate & Post-Graduate Courses

135/-

Big size, pp: 280

Secrets of Leadership

Insights from the **Panchatantra**

80/-

Demy size, pp: 136

Sure Success in Interviews

96/-

Demy size, pp: 152

QUIZ BOOKS

MATHEMATICS QUIZ BOOK

60/-

Demy size, pp: 216

Environment Quiz Book

48/-

Demy size, pp: 176

ASTRONOMY QUIZ BOOK

60/-

Demy size, pp: 208

BIRDS&ANIMALS QUIZ BOOK

60/-

Big size, pp: 128

Pre-School Primers

MY FIRST STEP OF
ALPHABET

NUMBERS

BIRDS AND ANIMALS

क ख ग

NURSERY RHYMES

VEGETABLES AND FRUITS

My first step of:
- Alphabet
- क • ख • ग
- Numbers
- Nursery Rhymes
- Birds & Animals
- Vegetables & Fruits

Price: Rs. **15/-** each

MEDICAL QUIZ BOOK

48/-

Demy size, pp: 192

Electronics & Computer Quiz Book

48/-

Demy size, pp: 260

HISTORY Quiz Book

60/-

Demy size, pp: 232

QUIZ TIME

80/-

Big size, pp: 208

PICTURE BOOK OF ALPHABETS

36/-

All books fully coloured and illustrated. Can be cleaned wiped off.

SCIENCE QUIZ BOOK

60/-

Demy size, pp: 192

GLOBAL Quiz Book

96/-

Demy size, pp: 256

4000 Quizzes

80/-

Big size, pp: 240

TAMIL NADU Quiz Book

40/-

Demy size, pp: 160

POSTAGE: RS. 15 TO 25/- EACH

YOGASANAS and SADHANA

Demy size, pp: 176
Also available in Hindi

Increase your HEIGHT

Demy size, pp: 112
Also available in Hindi

Ladies Slimming Course

Demy size, pp: 112
Also available in Hindi

Judo Karate

Demy size, pp: 128
Also available in Hindi

Sex Education Dictionary

Demy size, pp: 120

Body and Beauty Care

Big size, pp: 112

NATURE CURE at HOME

Demy size, pp: 200
Also available in Hindi

WEIGHT LOSS

Demy size, pp: 128

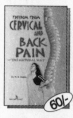

CERVICAL and BACK PAIN

Demy size, pp: 128

MOTHER-HOOD

Demy size, pp: 100

Reversing Aging

Demy size, pp: 224

Home Beauty Clinic

Big size, pp: 128
Also available in Hindi

SMOKING QUIT IT

Demy size, pp: 192

HEART Care

Demy size, pp: 120

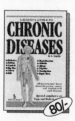

CHRONIC DISEASES

Demy size, pp: 176

FOOD Allergies

Demy size, pp: 126

Reveal your Glow

Demy size, pp: 124

HEALTH CHARTS & TABLES FOR YOU

Big size, pp: 144

SEXUAL PLEASURE

Demy size, pp: 160

FOODS that are Killing You

Demy size, pp: 144

Bowel Care The Natural Way

Demy size, pp: 112

HEART ATTACK

Demy size, pp: 152

I know what causes me allergy

Demy size, pp: 96

Herbal Beauty & Body Care

Big size, pp: 144
Also available in Hindi

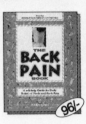

60/- | **96/-** | **80/-** | **60/-** | **175/-** | **96/-**

Demy size, pp: 120 | Demy size, pp: 192 | Demy size, pp: 128 | Demy size, pp: 144 | Big size, pp: 428 | Big size, pp: 228

80/- | | **68/-** | **88/-** | **120/-** | **110/-**

Demy size, pp: 152 | Vol-I: pp: 140 • Rs. 96/-
Vol-II: pp: 224 • Rs. 135/- | Demy size, pp: 128 | Demy size, pp: 224 | Big size, pp: 232 | Big size, pp: 152

48/- | **88/-** | **68/-** | **60/-** | **95/-** | **135/-**

Demy size, pp: 96 | Demy size, pp: 240 | Demy size, pp: 136 | Demy size, pp: 116 | Big size, pp: 224 | Big size, pp: 224

96/- | **80/-** | **80/-** | **68/-** | **135/-** | **96/-**

Demy size, pp: 224 | Demy size, pp: 224 | Demy size, pp: 120 | Demy size, pp: 136 | Big size, pp: 208 | Big size, pp: 184

HEALTH, BEAUTY CARE, HERBS & POPULAR SCIENCE

Demy size, pp: 248

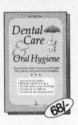
Demy size, pp: 136

Demy size, pp: 128

Demy size, pp: 128

Demy size, pp: 152

Big size, pp: 232

Demy size, pp: 184

Demy size, pp: 128

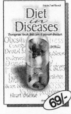
Demy size, pp: 104

Demy size, pp: 120

Demy size, pp: 132

Big size, pp: 1..

Big size, pp: 224

Big size, pp: 168

Big size, pp: 304

Big size, pp: 124

Demy size, pp: 96

Fact Books in Herbs

Discover the Amazi..
power of:
- Brahmi
- Ashwagandha
- Spirulina
- Vilayati Imli
- Salai guggal
- Amla

Demy s..
Price: Rs. **30/-** e..
Postage: 10/- each

Popular Science & Science Tricks

Big size • pp: 120
Also available in Hindi
(With CD)

Big size • pp: 196

Big size • pp: 120 each

Big size • pp: 104 each

Small Size
pp: 144

POSTAGE: RS. 15 TO 25/- EACH

10

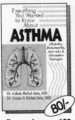
Everything You Wanted to Know About ASTHMA
Dr Ashok Mehul-Jain, MD
Dr Anuta A Mehul-Jain, MD
80/-
Demy size, pp: 168

Soul HEALING
Dr. Bruce Goldberg
88/-
Demy size, pp: 280

CHAKRA WORKOUT
For Body, Mind & Spirit
88/-
Demy size, pp: 240

Healing the Past For a Vibrant Future
68/-
Demy size, pp: 180

Dr. Bruce Goldberg
psychic attacks & evil spirits
96/-
Demy size, pp: 242

CHAKRA & KUNDALINI WORKBOOK
96/-
Demy size, pp: 264

A Beginner's Guide to ACUPRESSURE (SHIATSU Technique)
Using Japanese Finger Pressure for the Relief of Headaches, Back Pain, and Hypertension
36/-
Demy size, pp: 64

Auras
See Them in only 60 Seconds!
80/-
Demy size, pp: 144

Reiki
48/-
Demy size, pp: 104

TAOIST YOGA & CHI KUNG
Live over 100 years
120/-
Demy size, pp: 304

The Magic of Aromatherapy
108/-
Demy size, pp: 264

THE ACUPRESSURE HANDBOOK
135/-
Big size, pp: 264

COLOUR THERAPY
48/-
Demy size, pp: 84

the healing touch of Reiki
68/-
Demy size, pp: 112

MASTER APPROACHES TO NEW AGE ALTERNATIVE THERAPIES
80/-
Demy size, pp: 200

WATER A Miracle Therapy
68/-
Demy size, pp: 112

Magneto Therapy
The miraculous healing power
68/-
Demy size, pp: 128

THE PRACTICAL REIKI
HEALING THROUGH UNIVERSAL LIFE-FORCE ENERGY
96/-
Big size, pp: 168

The miracle of Music Therapy
80/-
Demy size, pp: 144

21 Power Tools of Reiki
A guide to awareness and practical skills
60/-
Demy size, pp: 136

Magic Therapy of COLOURS
Holistic healing through colours
60/-
Demy size, pp: 128

Healing Heart Disease Naturally
96/-
Demy size, pp: 200

Relaxation Techniques
195/-
Demy size, pp: 272

The Healing Power of MUDRAS
The Yoga of the hands
68/-
Demy size, pp: 112

POSTAGE: RS. 15 TO 25/- EACH

Rapidex PICTURE DICTIONARY
48/-
Big size, pp: 48
(In colour)

लोकोक्तियां (PROVERBS)
60/-
Demy size, pp: 136

Official Notings & Draftings
120/-
Big size, pp: 231

the children's picture dictionary
72/-
Big size, pp: 58
(In colour)

Interesting Stories to learn PROVERBS
72/-
Big size, pp: 98
(Double colour)

CHILDREN'S SCIENCE ENCYCLOPEDIA
380/-
Big size, pp: 520

Children's Library of Knowledge
360/-
Big size, pp: 384

OVER 300 GREAT LIVES
120/-
Demy size, pp: 344

The World's Greatest BLUNDERS That dramatically changed the history of mankind
60/-
Demy size, pp: 128

BABY RECORD & PHOTO ALBUM
100/-
Big size • pp: 52 (In 4 colou
Deluxe Binding
Also available in Hindi

THE HUTCHINSON CONCISE DICTIONARY of QUOTES
68/-
Demy size, pp: 352

THE HUTCHINSON CONCISE DICTIONARY of ENGLISH USAGE
50/-
Demy size, pp: 184

THE HUTCHINSON CONCISE DICTIONARY of SCIENCE
96/-
Demy size, pp: 456

2000 English Phrases & Sentences
60/-
Demy size, pp: 128

Many Faces of WORDS Word Power
24/-
Demy size, pp: 152

Rapidex Dictionary Of Spoken words with usages
60/-
Demy size, pp: 19(

SPICY SIDE OF SPEECHES FUN WITH ENGLISH
60/-
Demy size, pp: 128

The Funny side of ENGLISH A read-n-laugh manual to the English language
68/-
Demy size, pp: 232

POSTAGE: RS. 15 TO 20/- EACH

Bloomsbury Dictionaries

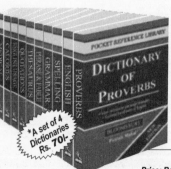

A set of 4 Dictionaries Rs. 70/-

- Dictionary of Phrase & Fable
- English Thesaurus
- Spelling Dictionary
- Dictionary of English Usage
- Medical Dictionary
- Dictionary of Calories
- English Dictionary*
- Dictionary of Grammar*
- Dictionary of Proverbs*
- Dictionary of Quotations*

Pocket size • Pages: 256
Price: Rs. **30/-** each • Postage: Rs. 10/- each

COMPUTER BOOKS

199/-
Also available in Hindi
Big size, pp: 520 (FREE CD-ROM, SMS Joke Book & Mouse Pad),

150/-
Big size, pp: 224
Also available in Hindi

Microsoft **Word 2000**
175/-
Big size, pp: 448

Microsoft **Windows 98**
195/-
Big size, pp: 520

THE **WAP BOOK**
95/-
Big size, pp: 144

Internet and e-mail
99/-
Big size, pp: 136

BASIC COMPUTER PROGRAMMING
68/-
Big size, pp: 264

Dreamweaver 3
195/-
Big size, pp: 360/-

COMPUTER FOR BEGINNERS
68/-
Big size, pp: 192

The **Java Book**
195/-
Big size, pp: 416

Low-cost Web Site
225/-
Big size, pp: 444

Internet Marketing & Promotions
225/-
Big size, pp: 392

Microsoft **FrontPage 98** in easy steps
90/-
Big size, pp: 184

Microsoft **Outlook 2000** in easy steps
125/-
Big size, pp: 252

How To Dotcom
Robert McG
140/-
Demy size, pp: 296

Strategy
120/-
Demy size, pp: 164

RAPIDEX Straight to the point series

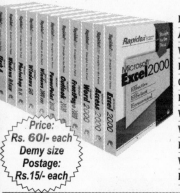

Microsoft Excel 2000
Access 2000
Word 2000
FrontPage 2000
Outlook 2000
PowerPoint 2000
Windows 2000 User
Windows 98
PhotoShop 5.5
WindowsNT4 User
Flash 4

Price: Rs. 60/- each
Demy size
Postage: Rs.15/- each

RAPIDEX Condensed Users Guides

Core Java 2
Windows NT Server 4
Java Script & VB Script
Windows NT 4 Workstation

Price: Rs. 140/- each
Big size
Pages: 216 to 316 each

13

FUN, FACTS, HUMOUR, MAGIC, MYSTERY & HOBBIES

Strange But True Facts
Over 292 amazing, amusing and unusual facts and photos
80/-
Demy size, pp: 184

FUN WITH NUMBERS
40/-
Demy size, pp: 115
also available in Hindi

101 BRAIN TEASERS
48/-
Demy size, pp: 152
also available in Hindi

Incredible but True
36/-
Demy size, pp: 112
also available in Hindi

501 FASCINATING FACTS
40/-
Demy size, pp: 104
also available in Hindi, Bangla, Kannada & Assamese

501 ASTONISHING FACTS
36/-
Demy size, pp: 115
also available in Hindi

How to solve Crossword Puzzles
60/-
Demy size, pp: 104

Amusing Anecdotes on Indian Red Tape
A compilation of hilarious moments in the lamentable and dreaded bureaucracy
80/-
Demy size, pp: 176

Rib-Tickling JOKES
48/-
Pages: 128

THE WORLD'S BEST PROFESSIONAL JOKES
60/-
Pages 120

MEDICAL JOKES & HUMOUR
48/-
Pages: 152

ARMOUR OF HUMOUR
Hilarious Mrithis and Smiles Armed with rib-tickling cartoons
40/-
Demy size, pp: 128

DEFT DEFINITIONS
48/-
Demy size, pp: 1

Amusing Encounters of Daily Life
True tales that will make you grin and guffaw
68/-
Demy size, pp: 124

The Funniest Tales of Mullah Nasruddin
The wittiest stories of the world's best-loved jester
48/-
Pages: 144
(Also in Hindi)

50 WITTIEST TALES OF BIRBAL
48/-
Pages: 120

UNWRITTEN -FLAWS- OF INDIAN BUREAUCRACY
295/-
Demy size, pp: 248
(Hardbound)

The Red Monster
60/-
Demy size, pp: 104

The Witches of Waitiki
68/-
Demy size, pp: 176

The Woman in White
80/-
Demy size, pp: 1

101 Magic Tricks
Fun to learn & perform
88/-
Big size, pp: 112
(Full colour book)

MAGIC FOR FUN
40/-
Demy size, pp: 112
also available in Hindi, Kannada and Marathi

MAGIC for CHILDREN
48/-
Demy size, pp: 124
also available in Hindi

MAGIC for YOU
40/-
Demy size, pp: 124
also available in Hindi,

HOW TO DRAW CARTOONS
60/-
Demy size, pp: 124
also available in Hindi

Drawing and Painting Course
60/-
Big size, pp: 120
also available in Hindi

POSTAGE: RS. 15 TO 25/- EACH

14

Religious & Spiritual Books

Hindu Rites, Rituals, Customs and Traditions
160/- Hardbound pp: 328

Pearls of Spiritual Wisdom
80/-
Demy size, pp: 158

DEHYPNOTIC MEDITATION
96/-
Demy size, pp: 132

Know the Vedas At a Glance
80/-
Demy size, pp: 136

The Yoga of GITA
80/-
Demy size, pp: 152

VEDA
80/-
Demy size, pp: 144

KNOW THE UPANISHADS
80/-
Demy size, pp: 120

Glory of Spiritual India
80/-
Demy size, pp: 224

50 BHAGAVAT GITA
75/-
Demy size, pp: 208

Vedantic Truth Revealed
48/-
Demy size, pp: 104

Furniture Catalogue, Gates, Grills, Windows, Railings....

New STEEL FURNITURE CATALOGUE
Hardbound **195/-**

NEW FURNITURE CATALOGUE
120/-

GATES, GRILLS, RAILING SETS
60/-

Window Grills & Rolling shutters
60/-

GATES, GRILLS, RAILINGS & STAIRCASES
90/-

How best to Plan & Build YOUR HOME
120/-

DESIGNS OF WINDOWS
60/-

DESIGNS OF GATES
60/-

DESIGNS OF RAILINGS
60/-

All in big size

16

World Famous Series

WORLD-FAMOUS DISCOVERIES
Discoveries

WORLD-FAMOUS 101 GREAT LIVES
Great Lives (3 vols.)

Strange Mysteries
Strange Mysteries

GHOSTS
Ghosts

GREAT TREASURES
Great Treasurers

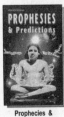
WORLD-FAMOUS Scientists
Scientists

World-Famous Unsolved Mysteries
Unsolves Mysteries

World-Famous Anecdotes
Anecdotes

WORLD-FAMOUS ADVENTURES
Adventures

Mythologies
Mythologies

PROPHESIES & Predictions
Prophecies & Predictions

Supernatural Mysteries
Supernatural Mysteries

FAMOUS INDIANS OF THE 20TH CENTURY
80/-
Famous Indians of 20th Century
Pages: 224

The World's greatest SEERS & PHILOSOPHERS
80/-
The World's Greatest Seers & Philosophers
Pages: 142

Demy size
Pages: 120-160 in each
Price: Rs. 48/- to 60/- each
Postage: 15/- each
Postage FREE on 6 or more books
All books in Hindi also
Four books in Bangla & Kannada